Matching
Major Eastern Hatches

Matching
Major Eastern Hatches

New Patterns for Selective Trout

Henry Ramsay

HEADWATER
BOOKS

STACKPOLE
BOOKS

To friends past and present who have shared their love of clear flowing waters and the bright speckled fish that dwell in them

Copyright © 2010 by Henry Ramsay

Published by
STACKPOLE BOOKS
5067 Ritter Road
Mechanicsburg, PA 17055
www.stackpolebooks.com

Photographs by the author except where noted

First edition

Library of Congress Cataloging-in-Publication Data

Ramsay, Henry, 1961–
    Matching major Eastern hatches : new patterns for selective trout / Henry Ramsay.
        p. cm.
    Includes bibliographical references and index.
    ISBN-13: 978-0-8117-0730-5
    ISBN-10: 0-8117-0730-X
  1. Fly tying. 2. Freshwater insects—East (U.S.) 3. Trout fishing—East (U.S.) I. Title.
    SH451.R25 2010
    799.17'57—dc22
                                        2010018946

Contents

Acknowledgments

To list all of the people who have in some way shaped, influenced, or supported this book would be a major undertaking as there have been many who deserve credit. Thanks go first and foremost to my Lord for blessing me with the opportunity to enjoy the sport of fly fishing all these years and for providing me with the chance to share it with others. Thank you to my family for their years of sacrifices and patience. Thank you to my mother for her kindness and understanding in raising a son obsessed with fly fishing and the outdoors. Thanks go to a list of departed friends, since moved on to fish better rivers, who provided instruction, inspiration, encouragement, and treasured memories: Henry Heil, Charles Brown, George Maurer, Ernest Schwiebert, and Jim Bashline. Thank you to a list of people for their companionship and friendship both on and off of the water, and for their advice, input, and support along the way: Gavin Robinson, Wes Osborne, Steve Spurgeon, Bud Hofer, Paul Weamer, Tony Gehman, and my daughter, Emily.

A special thank you goes to Barry and Cathy Beck for their wonderful photographic contributions and to Jay Nichols at Headwater/Stackpole Books for his willingness to bring this book to life and for his guidance and patience in putting it all together.

Introduction

As fly fishermen we hold trout with such high regard that we sometimes give them credit for intelligence and powers of reason far beyond what they deserve. Exerting our best attempts to fool them, carrying the best tackle we can afford, and casting flies we feel should be more than adequate to imitate the natural on cobweb-thin leaders, we can't help but presume that they possess significant intelligence. It's always difficult to accept the rejection of our best efforts and abilities by an organism equipped with a brain the size of a bean, but it's a daily occurrence on trout rivers everywhere.

Ernie Schwiebert wrote in his 1972 *Remembrances of Rivers Past* that "anglers are shaped by their rivers," and I think that is true. Every angler and fly tier is influenced by the waters that he fishes regularly. For some anglers that shaping process is the result of extensive travel to a wide range of watersheds; for others, it comes as a result of loving and learning a local stream and developing an intimate knowledge of its mysteries. My own shaping

The author fishes a Pocono Mountain stream in the early season. EMILY RAMSAY

Pennsylvania offers many opportunities for those who favor small mountain streams—like this Pocono stream—and the unique challenges they present. GAVIN ROBINSON

A nice brown trout in the net is a reward for reading the water, making a good fly selection, and presenting it to the trout with a well-placed cast. BARRY AND CATHY BECK

process has primarily occurred on the streams and rivers of Pennsylvania. The Keystone State's diversity reflects such a wide range of water types, hatches, and fishing situations that it is fertile proving grounds for solving fly-tying and fly-fishing problems.

Pennsylvania is the ideal state for match-the-hatch anglers. All of the classic mayfly hatches are found here as well as a wide array of caddisflies, stoneflies, and terrestrial insects. Hatches begin in the cold and blustery days of March and end in the brightly colored days of autumn. The more fertile watersheds host a rich abundance of fly life, at times producing multiple hatches that

increase the challenges. But perhaps more important are the types of streams that fishermen can enjoy and learn from. The state's trout waters vary from small, tumbling mountain brooks and pocketwater freestone streams born in the spring seeps of the hemlock- and laurel-covered mountains and hills of the Appalachians and the Poconos to the quiet meadows of the limestone spring creeks that emerge full-blown from the cool depths of large underground springs. Pennsylvania also has a number of larger freestone streams like Pine Creek and tailwater fisheries like the Lehigh and Delaware rivers that offer great trout fishing.

On the mountain streams, fish do not have long to scrutinize a meal or they will go hungry, and since food is often not abundant, fish can't afford to be choosy. For these fish, general patterns are adequate. Fish in the placid currents of the spring creeks, tailwaters, and larger

The Falling Spring Branch near Chambersburg, Pennsylvania, is a perfect example of a classic limestone stream with crystal clear water, complex currents, and extremely wary trout. Success in these types of difficult conditions depends on a stealthy approach, a perfect presentation, and a well-designed fly pattern.

freestone streams, however, are harder to catch. Higher fertility increases the number of organisms on which trout can feed and slower currents afford them better opportunity to scrutinize their food. The crystalline waters of the spring creeks of central Pennsylvania were the stream laboratories for Vince Marinaro and a group of innovative fly dressers who would, through a painstaking process of trial and error, present flies to fish they could observe and make subtle design changes based on the success of the patterns, many of which profoundly changed the way we approach imitating insects today.

In addition to the wide range of water types and multitude of hatches, another factor has influenced my choice of flies. Many of Pennsylvania's waters see considerable fishing pressure, particularly those that flow near populated parts of the state. On catch-and-release waters, the trout—stocked or wild—can develop selective feeding behaviors. Conditioned to anglers, the fish do not

flee after a botched cast, but they generally inspect their food closely before making a final decision. To catch these types of fish, a good presentation is often not enough. To ensure consistent success on the water, you must pair a perfect presentation with a good fly pattern.

Creating a good fly pattern for the rivers that I most often fish requires attention to the natural's coloration, profile, and size as well as the natural's behaviors, such as movement and its position in or on the water at each stage in its life cycle. Additionally, it is important to consider other, more subtle, qualities such as the distinct light patterns that each insect creates when it contacts the surface film of the water.

■ ■ ■

One of my favorite things to do after a morning of trout fishing is to stop and observe the fish from a

The beautiful North Branch of the Potomac River in western Maryland is a typical eastern tailwater river with abundant fly hatches and challenging fish.

bridge. Watching and studying the trout and their behavior is really an eye-opening experience, particularly when they are actively feeding. A wild trout, or even a stocked fish that's spent enough time in a stream, becomes a master of pattern recognition, rapidly deciding to take or reject something drifting in the current. The abundance of similar foods—such as when mayflies, midges, or caddis are hatching—only serves to enhance and reinforce this selectivity.

And the fish are not just learning about natural foods. Just consider the typical trout in a special-regulation stream that sees a steady parade of flies (both natural and artificial) and fishermen on a regular basis. After being caught and released on several occasions, the fish becomes quickly adept at recognizing counterfeit insects, even in the diminutive size 24 or 26 flies. Some of the more practiced trout drift back with the impostor to inspect it for a longer time.

Given that the trout has a brain the size of a bean, what makes a fly succeed or fail in fooling the fish, even when presentation is perfect? Finding the answer to this question has been my passion as a fly tier. My main goal has been to incorporate the primary characteristics unique to the insect I am imitating, particularly the light patterns created by the floating insect, the silhouette that it presents, the types of movement it may make, and its color. Along the way, I have tried and tied many patterns and styles of flies, the most successful of which I share in this book.

All of the fly patterns in this book are the result of years of experimentation, testing, and modification using various materials and designs to create fly patterns for pressured fish. Many of the patterns in this book introduce new concepts and tying techniques for imitating the insects that we see on our streams; others stem from previous fly patterns. The CDC Thorax Dun, for example, builds on the design of Vince Marinaro's unique pattern but uses a number of newer materials that weren't available or commonly used in Marinaro's day. The result is an effective imitation for difficult trout rising to mayfly duns wherever you find them. I hope Vince would approve.

The species-specific imitations and the color variations listed here are designed to match hatches on waters in the eastern United States, but over the span of nearly 30 years as a custom fly tier, I have provided flies to customers who have fished them successfully on streams and rivers all across the United States. Think of the patterns in this book as styles, or templates, that you can adapt to imitate insects on the rivers you fish. Nearly all mayfly duns, for example, have similar shapes, profiles, and footprints on the film of the water. The same goes for caddis and stonefly adults. Subsurface stages of aquatic insects such as caddisfly pupae and stoneflies also share many common physical attributes and behaviors. Change the colors and sizes to match those you see on the water you fish.

I hope you enjoy tying and fishing these patterns as much as I do. I also hope that they introduce to you a few new techniques to use at your tying bench and improve your success on the stream.

A wild brown trout rises to inspect a drifting insect. Fishermen for centuries have pondered which characteristics and qualities of the natural insects are important to the fish's decision making process and how to best imitate those qualities with the flies they tie. JAY NICHOLS

CDC Thorax Duns and Modernizing Marinaro

The thorax style of tie, even though increasingly popular, has not been fully appreciated.

VINCE MARINARO, *IN THE RING OF THE RISE*

The limestone streams of central Pennsylvania erupt as large springs from faults in the earth's surface. Flowing cold and clear through limestone marl deposits of calcium carbonate, these peculiar rivers have an extremely high level of fertility and alkalinity compared with their freestone cousins and support an astonishing level of life. These rich waters are almost totally unaffected by the influences of runoff, precipitation, drought, and seasonal temperatures. They remain at a consistent temperature year-round that stays within the optimal range for trout to feed and grow. Unlike turbulent freestoners, these streams flow like silken ribbons of clear water through deep channels between thick beds of vegetation—elodea, chara, and watercress—that create complex currents and make presenting a fly in a natural drag-free drift difficult. The trout in these little rivers exhibit an extreme wariness that frustrates most fishermen.

The character of the Letort Spring Run and its demanding fish was the primary classroom and laboratory for the collaborative work of Charles K. Fox and Vincent

The famous Letort Spring Run in Carlisle, Pennsylvania, was the testing grounds for legendary writer Vince Marinaro. The difficult trout in this spring creek inspired fresh approaches to the design of mayfly dun imitations.
BARRY AND CATHY BECK

A male Baetis *dun. Blue-Winged Olives are multibrooded mayflies that hatch several times each season, making them an important hatch on many streams.*

*Below: A male Hendrickson (*Ephemerella subvaria*) dun.*
JAY NICHOLS

*A male Light Cahill (*Stenacron interpunctatum*) dun.*

Above: A male Maccaffertium ithaca *dun.*

*A male Slate Drake (*Isonychia bicolor*) dun.*

Above: This selection of Thorax Duns imitates some of the common midseason mayfly hatches such as the Cahills, March Browns, and Attenella Olives. JAY NICHOLS

Goose biots are perfect for imitating smaller mayfly dun and spinner bodies with well-defined segmentation, as well as useful for creating tails and antennae on stonefly and other nymph imitations. They are much shorter than turkey biots and are more opaque as well. Smooth or ribbed segmented bodies can be created from these depending on how they are tied in and wrapped around the hook. Soaking goose biots in water or a dampened paper towel makes them more flexible before use. I prefer to use biots from Wapsi and TroutHunter.

Marinaro, who explored why trout react and feed the way they do. The origin of Marinaro's Thorax Dun, which he first describes in *A Modern Dry-Fly Code*, published in 1950, traces its root to an experience with three difficult fish on the Letort during a Sulphur hatch. These three browns were doing a good job of turning their noses at the conventional flies Marinaro was using at the time when at last he changed to a fly based on Edward Ringwood Hewitt's Neversink Skater, a fly that consisted only of an oversize hackle palmered over a dubbed body on a short-shank hook. Marinaro took each of the three browns on this fly, which made him wonder why this fly was more effective than those that he tried earlier. Mari-

naro summarizes his experience: "I am certain now that it can be explained on the basis that it had a good light pattern, not distorted by a long submerged body and tail, and a fairly good representation of the pale watery wing." The shortfall of the skater-type patterns, as Marinaro noted, is that the pattern often fails to stay perched upright on the water by the tips of its hackle-tip feet and is prone to fall over, ruining its light pattern.

To gain better balance and stability, Marinaro moved the wing and hackle closer to the hook's midpoint. Marinaro explains further: "Far more important to the trout is the presence of the fore body or thorax. Without exception, this part of the body hugs the surface of the

A mayfly dun with its upright wings presents a unique image when it enters the trout's window of vision, and Marinaro's studies determined this to be a primary trigger in initiating the rise of a feeding trout. Vince's thorax-style pattern made the wings the focal point of the fly. BARRY AND CATHY BECK

water closely, often times touching it. It is sometimes part of the light pattern beyond the circumference of the window and is most prominent in the window itself. As with the submerged body of the spinner which has broken through the mirror, it is startlingly clear in outline, and possibly in color, to the trout."

Much of Marinaro's writing minimizes coloration or matching mayfly species specifically; his highest priority for effective imitation was the light pattern created by the fly and the upright wings. Marinaro stresses that "moving the wings [of the thorax-style dun] to its proper place is not enough. If it must be given the full value that it deserves, something more than the conventional treatment is necessary. The standard tie for wings, with any of the usual materials, is patently defective in a number of ways. The starling and duck feathers are fragile things, depending for cohesion upon interlocking fibers, which are quickly rent apart by a few casts. Wood duck and hackle point wings make no pretense of maintaining shape and have the annoying property of becoming thin and wispy when they are wetted. They are sadly lacking in one great necessity, namely, width of wing as it exists

in the living dun and spinner." Marinaro preferred, in place of those traditional materials, matched wing pairs shaped from the lower webby portions of neck hackles or duck flank, which create a more defined silhouette.

Early dry flies developed for the calm chalkstreams of England had tails that were very sparse or lacked tails altogether, as discussed by authors such as Frederick Halford, J. W. Dunne, and Alfred Ronalds. To adapt dry flies to the more turbulent American rivers, tiers added long stiff tail fibers, which helped keep the body of the fly from contacting the surface and increasing the amount of tension in the surface film. Marinaro consented that tails were not imitative because the natural insects elevated their tails above the water's surface, but tails tied in a wide V shape did provide better balance and ensured the fly landed upright.

Marinaro theorized that a stiff collar of hackle wrapped in the conventional manner inhibited the ability to hook fish well, so he tied in a hackle by its stem between the wings of the fly and wound it diagonally in a crisscross pattern, first from front to back in one direction, then from back to front at an opposite angle. The end

This thorax-style March Brown pattern, the author's variation of the Marinaro Thorax Dun, replaces the wing post with CDC feathers and the abdomen of the fly with turkey or goose biots. JAY NICHOLS

result is interesting, but sadly it is difficult to execute in a way that looks neat and well tied. I wrap the hackle in open turns to expose the thorax region of the fly to the fish and trim the underside fibers in a wide V pattern. The original Marinaro pattern also excluded the abdominal portion of the body. While Marinaro may be correct in his argument that the trout never sees the body of a natural dun, I prefer to include the abdomen for aesthetics.

Though Vince Marinaro's design for the Thorax Dun never caught on with fishermen in his lifetime, at least not the way that he expected, it strongly influenced many of today's modern mayfly imitations. Marinaro's keen insights and willingness to experiment on the stream with often radically different approaches in a sport that prides itself so much on adherence to tradition paved the way for many of the features in contemporary fly designs.

My version of the Thorax Dun uses CDC feathers to form the wing rather than the cut wings that Marinaro preferred, making the fly float better and cast easier while still presenting a well-defined wing profile. I also use goose or turkey biots for the abdomen because I think they imitate the segmentation and waxy appearance of a

mayfly's abdomen better than dubbing. Turkey biots are the perfect choice for larger flies as they are much longer than goose biots and can be used for most of the big drake patterns as well as average-size flies. Goose biots work well for smaller flies. Hook choices vary from tier to tier, and for my mayfly duns and spinners, I use three styles from Daiichi, depending mostly on the size of the fly being tied. For imitations in sizes 12 to 18 I use the model 1100, which is a standard-length light wire hook, and I switch to the Daiichi 1180 for the smaller-size flies. The 1180 has a slightly larger eye for those of us who struggle with fine tippets in low-light conditions. For imitations of the larger mayflies such as the March Browns and Slate Drakes, I use the Daiichi 1260, a longer-shanked hook that reduces the hook gap on the larger flies.

The color of all mayfly duns varies considerably from stream to stream within any species. Modify the patterns presented here to match the flies on your favorite streams. It is important to capture specimens to be able to examine and closely match the underside coloration of the insects as the trout sees them.

TYING THE CDC THORAX DUN (MARCH BROWN)

MARCH BROWN
(*Maccaffertium vicarium*)

Hook:	#12-14 Daiichi 1260
Thread:	Tan 8/0 Uni-Thread
Tails:	Ginger Microfibetts
Abdomen:	Tan turkey biot
Thorax:	Tan Superfine dubbing
Wings:	Natural brown CDC and brown partridge fibers (optional)
Hackle:	Ginger and grizzly

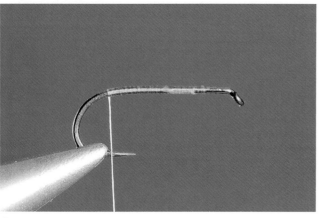

1. Clamp a dry-fly hook in the vise and attach tan 8/0 thread at the midpoint of the hook shank. Wrap the tying thread to a point over the end of the barb.

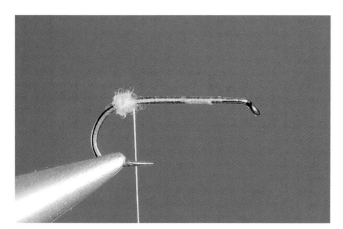

2. Apply tan Superfine dubbing to the thread and form a small dubbing ball at this point.

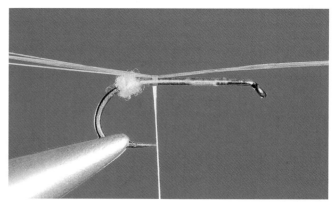

3. Select six ginger Microfibetts and tie in ⅛ inch in front of the dubbing ball. The tails should be 1 to 1½ times the length of the hook shank. Be sure to keep the fibers flat on the top of the hook shank. For flies on #12-14 hooks, use six tail fibers (three fibers per side), #16-22 use four tail fibers (two fibers per side), and #24-26 use two tail fibers (a single fiber per side).

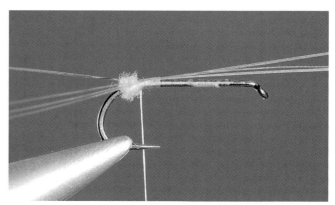

4. Wrap the thread back toward the dubbing ball. As you wrap, the fibers should naturally begin to separate. Divide them evenly on each side of the dubbing ball. Make a tight wrap against the base of the dubbing ball to lock the tails in position.

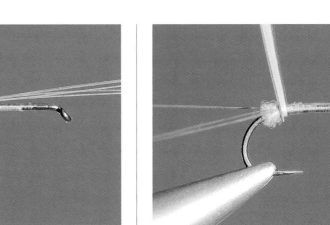

5. Tie a tan turkey biot in by the tip so that it is flat on the top of the hook shank and the edge with raised flue fibers is on the opposite side. Tying the biot in this way will create a heavily segmented body with a raised rib when you wrap the fiber. If you tie the biot in with the fuzzy edge toward you, you will create a smooth, segmented body.

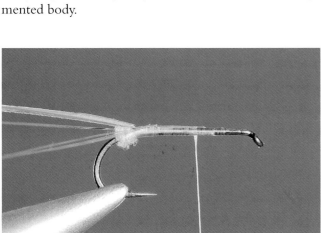

6. Trim the Microfibetts and wrap the tying thread forward two-thirds the length of the hook shank.

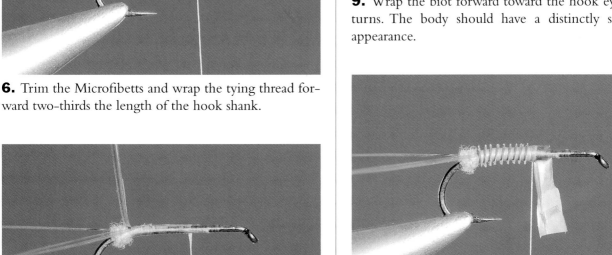

7. Grasp the base of the biot in your hackle pliers and pull upward, folding the biot so that the fuzzy edge is now oriented toward the tails of the fly.

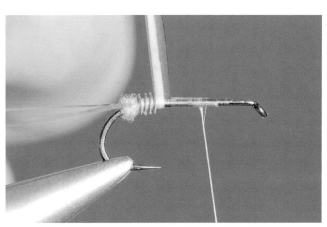

8. Take the first turn close against the base of the tail fibers.

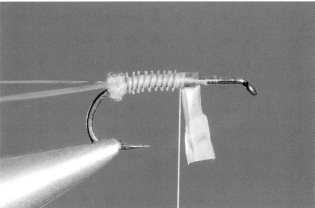

9. Wrap the biot forward toward the hook eye in even turns. The body should have a distinctly segmented appearance.

10. Wrap the biot forward to a point just beyond the center of the hook shank and tie it off.

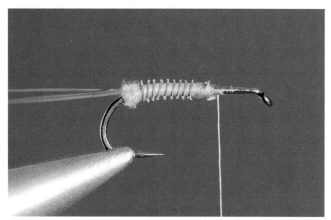

11. Trim off the excess biot fiber closely with scissors. Note that the completed abdomen should be even and free of any bumps or irregularities.

12. Select two full natural brown CDC feathers and stack them so that the tips are even. I prefer CDC from TroutHunter. Hold the paired feathers over the hook to determine the length, which should be equal to that of the hook shank. Grasp the feathers firmly with your left thumb and forefinger (if you are a right-handed tier) and hold them tightly against the top of the hook shank with the feather tips pointing forward over the hook eye. Take one loose turn of thread completely around the wing and pull tight. Take several more tight turns of thread.

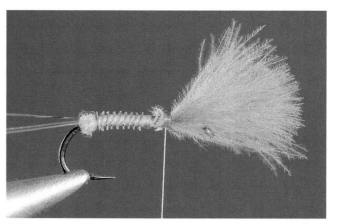

13. Trim the butts of the CDC feathers closely.

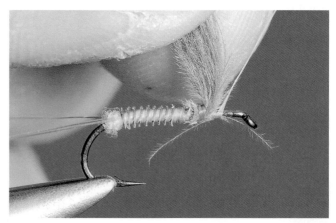

14. Post the wing by pulling it upright and taking turns of thread in front of it. Hold the wing by the tips and wrap upward for 1/16 inch, then back down to the hook shank.

15. The posted wing should appear like this when completed.

16. Select a large brown partridge hackle and cut a notch in the tip. This is an optional step that I like to add for many of the mayfly duns that have speckled or mottled wings such as the March Browns or Light Cahills.

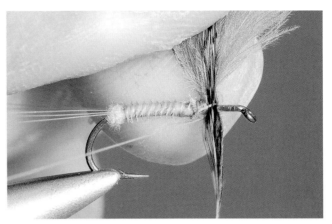

19. Take two loose diagonal turns of tying thread around the folded hackle before pulling the thread taut. This will help to distribute the partridge fibers more evenly.

17. Bring the hackle against the wing from the underside of the fly.

20. When thread tension is applied the fibers should fan slightly

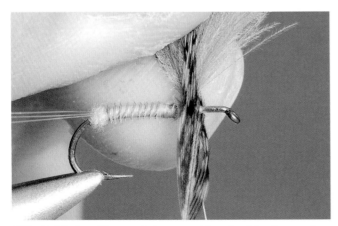

18. Fold the fibers of the partridge hackle flat against the sides of the CDC and hold them there with your left hand.

21. Hold the wing fibers tightly against the CDC post with your left thumb and forefinger and take a few turns of thread around the base of the wing post.

22. Return the tying thread to a position behind the wing.

23. Select a cree hackle with barbs 1 to 1½ times the width of the hook gap and strip off the webby base fibers. You can also use one grizzly and one ginger hackle. Tie in the stem of the hackle firmly, leaving ⅛ inch of clear stem exposed. Orient the bright side of the hackle toward the hook eye. Trim away the excess stem.

24. Dub the first half of the thorax with tan Superfine dubbing.

25. Dub in front of the wing, stopping well short of the hook eye. Be sure to dub tightly against the base of the wing post to secure it in an upright position and to cover any areas directly under it.

26. Wrap the hackle forward in open turns over the thorax section and tie off.

27. Trim away the surplus hackle tip.

28. Dub a small head of tan Superfine dubbing, whip-finish, and trim the thread closely.

29. Rotate the vise and trim the hackle fibers flat on the underside of the fly.

30. The completed March Brown CDC Thorax Dun. The techniques used here produce a fly that floats very well and sits close to the surface, giving the fish the well-defined silhouette of a freshly hatched mayfly dun.

GORDON QUILL
(*Epeorus pleuralis*)

Hook:	#12 Daiichi 1100
Thread:	Yellow 8/0 Uni-Thread
Tails:	Dark gray Microfibetts
Abdomen:	Black-and-white barred turkey biot dyed light yellow
Thorax:	Callibaetis Superfine dubbing
Wings:	Natural dun CDC
Hackle:	Bronze dun

EARLY BLUE QUILL
(*Paraleptophlebia adoptiva*)

Hook:	#16-18 Daiichi 1100
Thread:	Dark brown 8/0 Uni-Thread
Tails:	Dark gray Microfibetts
Abdomen:	Mahogany turkey or goose biot
Thorax:	Mahogany brown Superfine dubbing
Wings:	Natural dun CDC
Hackle:	Bronze dun

RED QUILL FEMALE
(*Ephemerella subvaria*)

Hook:	#12-14 Daiichi 1100
Thread:	Dark brown 8/0 Uni-Thread
Tails:	Dark gray Microfibetts
Abdomen:	Rusty brown turkey biot
Thorax:	Rusty brown Superfine dubbing
Wings:	Natural dun CDC
Hackle:	Bronze dun

HENDRICKSON
(*Ephemerella subvaria*, male)

Hook:	#12-14 Daiichi 1100
Thread:	Tan 8/0 Uni-Thread
Tails:	Dark gray Microfibetts
Abdomen:	Hendrickson turkey biot
Thorax:	Hendrickson pink Superfine dubbing
Wings:	Natural dark dun CDC
Hackle:	Bronze dun

LIGHT CAHILL
(*Maccaffertium ithaca, M. modestum,* and *Stenacron interpunctatum*)

Hook:	#14-16 Daiichi 1100
Thread:	Light cahill 8/0 Uni-Thread
Tails:	Cream Microfibetts
Abdomen:	Light cahill turkey biot
Thorax:	Light cahill Superfine dubbing
Wings:	Cream CDC and gray partridge fibers (optional)
Hackle:	Cream or barred cream

LEMON CAHILL
(*Stenacron* spp.)

Hook:	#14-16 Daiichi 1100
Thread:	Light cahill 8/0 Uni-Thread
Tails:	Yellow Microfibetts
Abdomen:	Sulphur yellow turkey biot
Thorax:	Sulphur yellow Superfine dubbing
Wings:	Sulphur yellow CDC
Hackle:	Cream or barred cream

PALE SULPHUR
(*Ephemerella dorothea dorothea, E. invaria,* and *Leucrocuta hebe*)

Hook:	#14-18 Daiichi 1100
Thread:	Light cahill 8/0 Uni-Thread
Tails:	Yellow Microfibetts
Abdomen:	Yellow turkey or goose biot
Thorax:	Sulphur yellow Superfine dubbing
Wings:	Dyed light dun CDC
Hackle:	Honey dun or pale ginger

ORANGE SULPHUR
(*Ephemerella dorothea dorothea* and *E. invaria*)

Hook:	#14–18 Daiichi 1100
Thread:	Light cahill 8/0 Uni-Thread
Tails:	Yellow Microfibetts
Abdomen:	Sulphur orange turkey or goose biot
Thorax:	Sulphur orange Superfine dubbing
Wings:	Dyed light dun CDC
Hackle:	Cream dyed light pastel orange or honey dun

DARK BAETIS OLIVE

Hook:	#18–22 Daiichi 1180
Thread:	Olive dun 8/0 Uni-Thread
Tails:	Olive Microfibetts
Abdomen:	BWO goose biot
Thorax:	BWO Superfine dubbing
Wings:	Natural dun CDC
Hackle:	Grizzly dyed golden olive

Note: Use olive 14/0 Sheer for smaller sizes.

LIGHT BAETIS OLIVE

Hook:	#18–22 Daichii 1180
Thread:	Olive dun 8/0 Uni-Thread
Tails:	Olive Microfibetts
Body:	Olive goose biot
Thorax:	Olive Superfine dubbing
Wings:	Natural dun CDC
Hackle:	Grizzly dyed golden olive

Note: Use olive 14/0 Sheer for smaller sizes.

ATTENUATA OLIVE
(*Attenella attenuata*)

Hook: #16 Daiichi 1100
Thread: Light olive 8/0 Uni-Thread
Tails: Dark gray Microfibetts
Abdomen: Light olive turkey biot
Thorax: Golden olive Superfine dubbing
Wings: Natural dark dun CDC
Hackle: Cream dyed golden olive or dark blue dun

DARK LATA OLIVE
(*Drunella lata*)

Hook: #12-14 Daiichi 1100
Thread: Olive 8/0 Uni-Thread
Tails: Dark gray Microfibetts
Abdomen: Olive turkey biot
Thorax: Olive Superfine dubbing
Wings: Natural dun CDC
Hackle: Medium dun

SLATE DRAKE
(*Isonychia bicolor*)

Hook: #12-14 Daiichi 1260
Thread: Wine 8/0 Uni-Thread
Tails: Dark gray Microfibetts
Abdomen: Trico turkey biot
Thorax: Mahogany brown Superfine dubbing
Wings: Natural dun CDC
Hackle: Dark dun

YELLOW QUILL
(*Epeorus vitreus*)

Hook:	#14-16 Daiichi 1100
Thread:	Light cahill 8/0 Uni-Thread
Tails:	Dark gray Microfibetts
Abdomen:	Amber turkey biot
Thorax:	Amber Superfine dubbing
Wings:	Natural dark dun CDC
Hackle:	Dark dun

GREEN DRAKE
(*Ephemera guttulata*)

Hook:	#8-10 Daiichi 1260
Thread:	Light cahill 8/0 Uni-Thread
Tails:	Black moose hair
Abdomen:	Cream turkey biot
Thorax:	Light cahill Superfine dubbing
Wings:	Olive dyed CDC and olive dyed guinea or teal flank fibers
Hackle:	Grizzly dyed pale olive

BROWN DRAKE
(*Ephemera simulans*)

Hook:	#10-12 Daiichi 1260
Thread:	Tan 8/0 Uni-Thread
Tails:	Black moose hair
Abdomen:	Callibaetis turkey biot
Thorax:	Dark tan Superfine dubbing
Wings:	Natural brown CDC and dark brown partridge fibers
Hackle:	Cree or grizzly and brown mixed

2

The DNA Spinner

In tying the spinner we are confronted by vast difficulties, which make the tying of a dun seem comparatively easy.

<small>VINCE MARINARO, *A MODERN DRY FLY CODE*</small>

Trout hold their secrets close. The best fishermen on any stream don't necessarily carry the best tackle or have perfect casting technique. They have developed better observation and interpretation skills than their fellow anglers, and that trait alone separates them from the rest of us.

One late June evening, I slipped into my waders and vest and stood for a few minutes at the edge of a little river, watching the water and the air above it while I strung my rod. The surface was calm and very little air stirred the leaves of the trees; here and there the dimpling rises of feeding fish broke the calmness of the water. There were only a few speckled *Hydropsyche* caddisflies in the air. I was disappointed, but it was still early in the evening.

To pass the time I decided to fish a nymph pattern rather than wait for the flies to begin to hatch. I knotted a small caddis larva imitation to the tippet, added weight to the leader, and began drifting it in a deep seam in a current that usually held fish. Only one average-size trout took the nymph during the next half hour of casting.

DNA Frosty Fish Fiber, a thin–diameter synthetic fiber that was originally developed as a saltwater streamer material, has the perfect balance of stiffness and softness for spent spinner wings.
JAY NICHOLS

A selection of DNA spinners tied to match some of the common midseason hatches. JAY NICHOLS

Here and there more adult caddis began to appear, and the fish began to rise with increased frequency. I removed the caddis larva and changed it to an adult with CDC wings. The little sedge pattern drew little interest from a surprising number of fish. After another half hour of fruitless casting, I moved upstream toward the head of the long pool where other trout were working under the limbs of the overhanging hemlocks. These fish were no more cooperative than those downstream, totally ignoring the dry fly attached to my leader in favor of something that was obviously escaping my eyes.

As the sun settled behind the backdrop of trees, I finally crouched low to study the film on the water for clues. In short time, it all became clear to me—the surface was peppered with small, spent *Ephemerella dorothea* spinners. There was obviously a fall of spinners in progress farther upstream in the faster riffles, and the spent and dying spinners were easier to feed on than the fast-emerging caddisflies that had previously stolen my

attention. I chose a small #18 Sulphur spinner, touched its body and wings with floatant, and cast softly to the closest rising fish. The corresponding rise was the classic head to tail, and I tightened the line when I saw the rainbow's mouth engulf the fly. At the sting of the little hook, it bolted, and I kept the rod low and to the side to keep it away from the other rising fish. I took several more trout on the spinner pattern before it became too dark to follow the little fly's drift any longer. Finally solving the riddle that evening felt deeply satisfying.

In this particular case, I failed to observe the specific riseforms of the fish. In my own mind, the presence of adult caddis in the air and the rising fish equaled fishing an adult caddis imitation, and I didn't consider the other obvious clues. Trout feeding on hatching or ovipositing caddis usually exhibit showy rises that are often fast paced and splashy due to the fast emergence of these insects. Conversely, trout feeding on dying or spent spinners feed in slow rhythms taking the flies with quiet,

A nice brown trout in the net. The rises of spinner-feeding trout are often misread by anglers, and the drifting flies in the surface film can be hard to detect without close observation. BARRY AND CATHY BECK

relaxed rises that often faintly dimple the surface. With actively feeding trout the pace of the fish's feeding behavior often matches the pace of the food form being taken at the time. In this particular situation the riseforms did not match the insects that were most active at the time and failure to study the water and the behavior of the fish for more subtle clues yielded poor results.

Of all of the aquatic insects and the different stages of each involved that we imitate with our flies, the mayfly spinner or imago stage receives the least consideration from fishermen, with the diminutive spinners of the *Tricorythodes* species probably being the lone exception to this rule due to their long emergence period and the sheer quantity of spinners that fall to the water. In my years as a custom fly tier, I've tied many orders for mayfly nymph and dun imitations, caddis adults, larvae and pupae, terrestrials, and midges for my customers, but I would say that the fly category ignored more than any other by most fishermen is the mayfly spinner imitation. For the observant angler who recognizes the behavior and presence of spinner-feeding trout and is prepared to fish those situations on the stream with good imitations, the results are often spectacular. While most fishermen pay close attention to what is hatching on the water,

falling spinners often go unnoticed as many anglers associate the rising activity of fish they see with the flies that are hatching at the time. Spinners can be falling on the water from farther upstream and go undetected because we don't see the activity of the flies over the water. Floating low and prone on the surface, many spinners are difficult to see and require us to pay closer attention to detect their presence.

The mayfly spinner, or imago, is the final stage of the mayfly life cycle. After having spent most of the year in the water as a nymph crawling about the streambed, it swims to the surface when mature and emerges as an air-breathing subimago, or dun. In the final stage of the life cycle the dun molts into a spinner and then mates and returns to the water to deposit its eggs and start the process over again. During this process the dun undergoes a dramatic transformation. The body of the spinner now takes on a bright and shiny appearance after having shed the skin of the dun stage. Later in the hatch when the spinners have mated and returned to the water, many of them will have lost much of their body proteins and egg masses making their abdomens appear partially transparent. Vince Marinaro tried to mimic this effect on his larger imitations by tying extended bodies from

A male Baetis *species spinner.*

Below: A male Summer Blue Quill (Paraleptophlebia mollis) *spinner.*

*A female Little Yellow Quill (*Leucrocuta hebe*) spinner.*

Above: A male Light Cahill (Stenacron interpunctatum) *spinner.*

*A male Slate Drake (*Isonychia bicolor*) spinner.*

A Rusty DNA Spinner, floating flush on the stream surface, duplicates the profile and light pattern of a spent mayfly spinner.

porcupine quill sections that had the inner pith removed. He also used dubbing materials to create the best illusion of transparency, preferring natural seal fur above all others.

Perhaps the largest change resulting from this molting process is in the appearance of the wings. The wings of the dun stage that were dull shades of gray and other tones become clear or hyaline in coloration and shiny, reflecting the available light and making the mating swarms of spinners appear to sparkle in the air over the water. As the spinners complete their life cycle by returning to the water to deposit their eggs, the position of their wings changes in appearance to the fish as well. When the duns first emerged and drifted along on the surface before becoming airborne, they held their wings in an upright position, closed together. Now at the ends of their lives, the spinners land on the water with their wings spread outward. Sometimes this is in a nearly upright arrangement (semi-spent), other times the entire fly lands on its side, and at other times it drifts with the wings totally flat (spent). To the trout the image of a dun

is radically different from a spinner due to the wing positions of the respective life-cycle stages.

If you closely examine the wings of a dun or spinner, you'll notice small pleats that run the length of the wing from the base to the tips, making the wings in cross section appear to be corrugated or ridged like a washboard. Duns and spinners both have these deep folds in the wing, and while it is not important to replicate them in your duns because the fish do not see them, it's a totally different story with the spinner. All floating objects press into the meniscus of the surface film of the water wherever they make contact with it. These deflections of the film alter the penetration or reflection of the available light rays (refraction), producing a light pattern when viewed from below the surface. The ridged wings touch the film far differently than a flat object will. A flat object prevents light from penetrating through it. Even a transparent object, when flat, sometimes diffuses the available light, depending on the angle, and in other cases reflects it back upward, thereby creating for the trout's view an outline or silhouette of the shape involved. The spinner wing's creased cross section touches the surface at a number of points, creating a series of deflections in the surface film that appear as a bright sparkling light to the trout.

Constructing spinner wings with materials that actually touch the surface in the same way as the natural is an important consideration in an effective imitation. Duplicating only the translucence or wing profile alone doesn't go far enough. A good spinner pattern needs to possess not only the right shape and color of the natural mayfly wing, but also the correct texture and the right physical properties to interplay with light and the water surface in the same way that the natural wing of the spinner does.

Many fly tiers prefer synthetic yarns, and flies dressed with these materials are easy to tie and float well; however, some of these yarn-type materials lack the translucency, sparkle, and stiffness to make a really good imitation. I've experimented with a number of these and prefer the Z-Lon yarns over the polypropylene and Antron types for spent wings in the smallest spinner patterns. McFlylon is another interesting synthetic that is gaining popularity for posted mayfly wings, parachutes, and spent-wing spinners. The better materials, trilobal in cross section, have a slightly stiffer rather than a round profile and reflect better than the other types. Various film-type materials look great on spinners in the vise or the hand, but these spinners don't cast or fish well due to their tendencies to twist tippets and their failure to reproduce the correct trigger image for the fish.

Z-Lon fibers, Darlon, or Organza create a good, light pattern, float well when treated with a good paste floatant or preening oil, and do not twist delicate tippets. For my larger patterns (#8-20) I use a synthetic fiber designed and marketed for the saltwater fly-tying market called DNA Frosty Fish Fiber. I was introduced to this material by Ted Patlen, a great tier from New Jersey, and the credit goes to him for adapting it for spent mayfly wings. It perfectly imitates the natural spinner wing by having just the right degree of stiffness to hold its shape

in casting and use, and it creates the surface tension needed to keep the fly in the surface film. The material's fiber diameter is perfect for most of the commonly used spinner sizes, and its texture has a subtle crimping. Most importantly, it has a beautiful sparkly finish that reflects light well, simulating the light pattern of a spinner's wing with its pleated surfaces, and creates an illusion of translucency. For flies #8 and 10, I use seven or eight fibers, for #12 and 14, five strands, and on #16 and smaller flies, I use four. This provides enough wing material to create a wide-wing profile without making it too bulky or stiff to cast well.

When tying in the wings, the most important step is to flatten the wing fiber bunches at the bases of each wing. This is critical to achieve a flattened fan effect in the finished wing. Using a pair of smooth-jawed hemostats or needle-nose pliers, flatten the wing fiber bundles on each side, at the base of the fibers, to spread and compress the fibers into a flat plane. Touch the base of the wings with a clear head cement to hold them in this position. As in the mayfly dun imitations, I use three hook models from Daiichi with the fly size dictating which one is used. The larger flies such as the March Browns and Slate Drakes are tied on the model 1260 long-shank hook. The flies sized from #12 to 18 are tied on the model 1100, while for the smaller patterns I switch to the model 1180, which has a larger eye.

The last important consideration in dressing spinner patterns is the body of the fly. The mayfly spinner at this point in its life cycle is exhausted, starved, and just about out of gas, drifting helplessly in the surface film of the water. In the dun stage, the fly was a freshly hatched, vigorous insect that carried its tails, wings, and the end of its abdomen in the air. Now spent by all of its activity, it lies flat on the surface, all of its features and the coloration of its body and thorax visible to the trout in complete detail, totally undistorted and relatively free of the effects of refraction. A biot body is the perfect choice for imitating the distinct segmentation of the abdomen.

TYING THE DNA SPINNER (RUSTY)

RUSTY
**(*Ephemerella subvaria, Epeorus pleuralis,*
 and other spp.)**

Hook: #12-18 Daiichi 1100
Thread: Rusty brown 8/0 Uni-Thread
Tails: Dark dun Microfibetts
Abdomen: Rusty brown turkey or goose biot
Thorax: Rusty brown Superfine dubbing
Wings: Shrimp DNA Frosty Fish Fiber

Note: You can imitate the yellow egg sacs of the
female spinners of *E. subvaria* with a small ball of
sulphur yellow Superfine dubbing to separate the tail
fibers into their forked position.

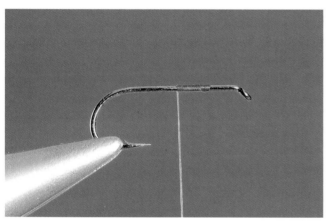

1. Clamp a dry-fly hook in the vise and attach rusty
brown 8/0 thread at the midpoint.

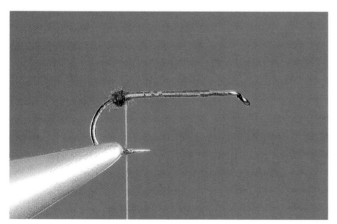

2. Wrap the tying thread toward the hook bend, stopping at a point over the end of the hook barb. Apply a
small amount of rusty brown Superfine dubbing and
form a small ball on the hook.

3. Select six dark dun Microfibetts.

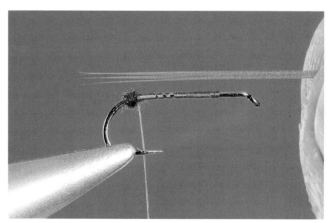

4. Gauge the length of the tail fibers. They should be
1½ times the length of the hook shank.

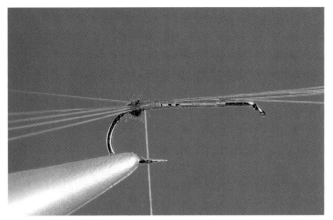

5. Tie in the tails on top of the shank, beginning approximately ⅛ inch forward of the dubbing ball. Wrap back over the tails to divide them, and separate the fibers into even bunches. Make the last turn of thread tight against the dubbing ball to keep them in place.

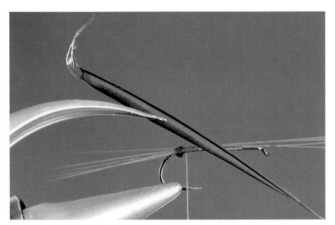

6. Select a rusty brown turkey biot.

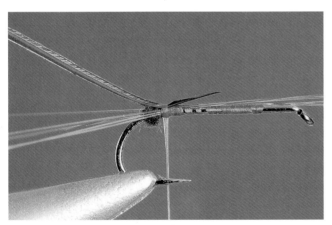

7. Tie the biot in by the tip so that it is flat on the top of the hook shank and the edge with the raised flue is on the side opposite you.

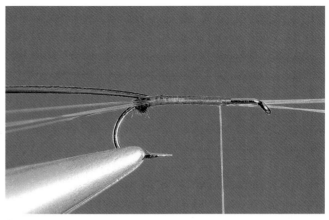

8. Wrap the tying thread forward toward the eye, stopping three-fourths of the way and wrapping over the butts of the tail fibers.

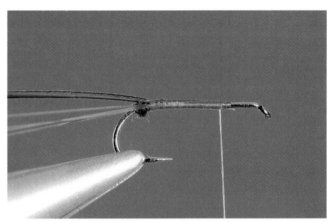

9. Trim the butts of the tail fibers closely.

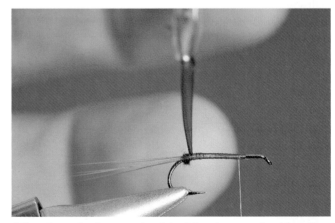

10. Place the butt end of the biot in your hackle pliers and lift it so that it is perpendicular to the hook shank. Orient the edge of the biot with the raised flue toward the hook bend.

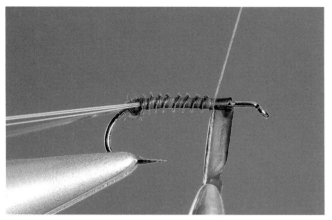

11. Wrap the biot forward in even turns for three-fourths of the hook shank and tie it off. Because the biot is tied in with the raised flue toward the hook bend, the body has raised segments.

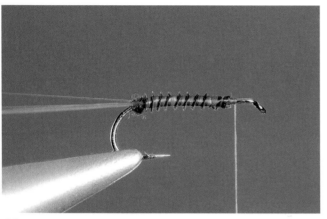

12. Trim off the surplus biot and wrap the tying thread halfway to the eye.

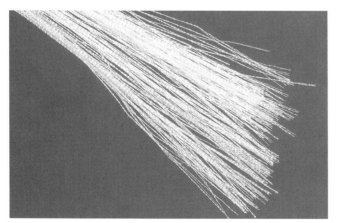

13. Select the appropriate number of fibers from a hank of DNA Frosty Fish Fibers to make the wings. For a size 14 spinner use five fibers.

14. Fold the group of fibers in half, then in half again, and hold them in this folded state.

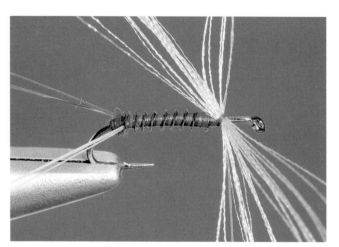

15. Tie the group of fibers to the hook shank, beginning with two diagonal turns and then several firm figure-eight wraps.

16. The DNA fibers should now be perpendicular to the hook shank. Do not trim the fibers yet.

17. Apply rusty brown Superfine dubbing to the thread and build a thorax by making figure-eight turns around the bases of the wings.

20. Trim the wing fibers so that they are equal to the length of the hook shank.

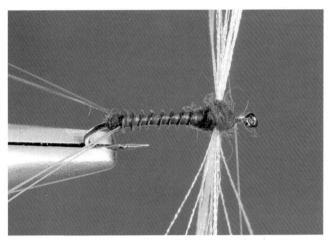

18. The dubbed thorax should be twice the diameter of the abdomen.

21. Use needle-nose pliers or hemostats with smooth jaws to flatten the wings close to the thorax so that the fibers spread into a wide fan.

19. Make a small head with thread and whip-finish.

22. Apply a small drop of head cement to the bases of the wings to fan the fibers.

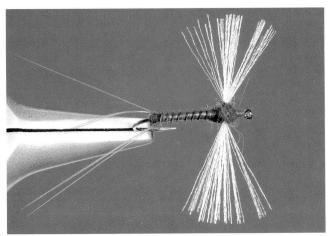

23. The finished fly emphasizes the well-defined segmentation and thick thorax of a natural spinner, but most importantly it closely matches the bright sparkling effect created by surface refraction where the wings come into contact with the surface of the water.

GOLDEN
(*Maccaffertium terminatum, Ephemerella dorothea dorothea, Epeorus vitreus, Leucrocuta hebe*)

Hook:	#12-18 Daiichi 1100
Thread:	Light cahill 8/0 Uni-Thread
Tails:	Light yellow Microfibetts
Abdomen:	Yellowish tan turkey or goose biot
Thorax:	Amber Superfine dubbing
Wings:	Shrimp DNA Frosty Fish Fiber

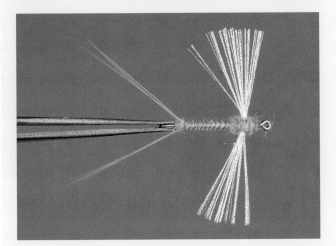

GREAT RED
(*Maccaffertium vicarium*)

Hook:	#12-14 Daiichi 1260
Thread:	Rusty brown 8/0 Uni-Thread
Tails:	Ginger Microfibetts
Abdomen:	Dark tan turkey biot
Thorax:	Ginger variant Superfine dubbing
Wings:	Shrimp DNA Frosty Fish Fiber

PALE SULPHUR
(*Ephemerella dorothea dorothea*)

Hook:	#14-18 Daiichi 1100
Thread:	Light cahill 8/0 Uni-Thread
Tails:	Cream Microfibetts
Abdomen:	Light cahill turkey or goose biot
Thorax:	Sulphur orange Superfine dubbing
Wings:	Shrimp DNA Frosty Fish Fiber

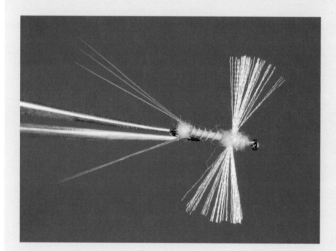

CREAM
(*Stenacron interpunctatum, Maccaffertium ithaca* and *modestum, Anthopotamus distinctus*)

Hook:	#12-16 Daiichi 1100
Thread:	Light cahill 8/0 Uni-Thread
Tails:	Cream Microfibetts
Abdomen:	Light cahill turkey or goose biot
Thorax:	Light cahill Superfine dubbing
Wings:	Shrimp DNA Frosty Fish Fiber

DARK MAHOGANY
(*Isonychia* spp., *Paraleptophlebia adoptiva*)

Hook:	#12 Daiichi 1260 and #12 to 18 Daiichi 1100
Thread:	Dark brown 8/0 Uni-Thread
Tails:	Dark dun Microfibetts
Abdomen:	Mahogany turkey or goose biot
Thorax:	Mahogany brown Superfine dubbing
Wings:	Shrimp DNA Frosty Fish Fiber

OLIVE BROWN
(*Attenella attenuata*, *Drunella lata*, and various Baetidae family olives)

Hook:	#12-22 Daiichi 1100 or 1180
Thread:	Dark brown 8/0 Uni-Thread
Tails:	Brown Microfibetts
Abdomen:	Olive turkey or goose biot
Thorax:	Brown olive Superfine dubbing
Wings:	Shrimp DNA Frosty Fish Fiber

BAETIS
(*Baetis* spp.)

Hook:	#18-22 Daichii 1180
Thread:	Cinnamon 14/0 Sheer
Tails:	Dark dun Microfibetts
Body:	BWO goose biot
Thorax:	Brown olive Superfine dubbing
Wings:	Shrimp DNA Frosty Fish Fiber

SUMMER BLUE QUILL MALE
(*Paraleptophlebia mollis*)

Hook:	#18 Daiichi 1100
Thread:	Dark brown 8/0 Uni-Thread
Tails:	White Microfibetts
Abdomen:	White goose biot
Thorax:	Mahogany Superfine dubbing
Wings:	Shrimp DNA Frosty Fish Fiber

Note: The Summer Blue Quill male spinner has a distinct dark tip on its abdomen. Use the same mahogany-colored dubbing to separate the tail fibers into a wide V.

BROWN DRAKE
(*Ephemera simulans*)

Hook: #10-12 Daiichi 1260
Thread: Tan 8/0 Uni-Thread
Tails: Four dark moose hairs
Abdomen: Tan turkey biot
Thorax: Tan Superfine dubbing
Wings: Smoke DNA Frosty Fish Fiber
Hackle: Cree or furnace tied parachute style on a post above the wings

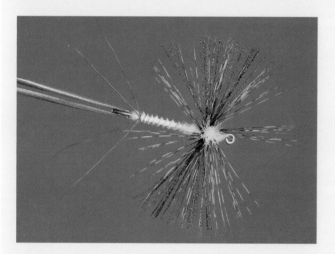

GREEN DRAKE
(*Ephemera guttulata*)

Hook: #8-10 Daiichi 1260
Thread: White 8/0 Uni-Thread
Tails: Four dark moose hairs
Abdomen: White turkey biot
Thorax: White Superfine dubbing
Wings: Black DNA Frosty Fish Fiber
Hackle: Silver badger or dark pardo coq de Leon or dark grizzly tied parachute style on a post above the wings

3

The Emerging Dun

There is a period, however, when the mayfly's appearance and behavior do not conform to any of these stages.

RENÉ HARROP, *TROUTHUNTER*

𝓘n the early stages of a hatch, there is a sudden change in the activity of the nymphs that have spent the past year crawling about the stones, gravel, and weeds of the streambed. Mature nymphs ready to hatch into adult air-breathing insects migrate toward shallower water on many streams to make it easier to reach the water's surface. Their wing cases are full due to the completely developed wings held within them, and the wing cases will often be nearly black. As the day's hatch begins, these nymphs leave the security of the streambed, many drifting for considerable distances before they finally reach the film.

Nymphs such as those that belong to *Maccaffertium* and *Ephemerella* struggle to reach the surface while others such as those of the genus *Isonychia* and *Baetis* are fast swimmers that reach the surface quickly. As this activity heightens and nymphs begin to reach the surface film in good numbers, so do the fish that are actively pursuing them. As the adults emerge, many feeding fish, especially smaller ones, will switch from eating nymphs to eating freshly hatched duns as they drift on the surface before flying to the safety of the streamside foliage. Larger trout will often shun making the transition to feeding on adult insects and will instead focus on emerging nymphs that

The Almost Dun is a good imitation of an emerging or crippled mayfly dun.
JAY NICHOLS

Above: A well-prepared fly box should contain a selection of flies to imitate the hatches you are likely to encounter. In this picture are a variety of emerger patterns that match March Browns and the Attenella Olives. JAY NICHOLS

An assortment of emerger and cripple patterns for matching the Sulphur hatch. Often a high number of Sulphurs are stillborn or crippled during emergence. JAY NICHOLS

are swimming or drifting. This is not always true, but as a general rule most large trout tend to prefer the safety of feeding subsurface, and you can increase your chances of catching them by fishing emergers during most of the mayfly hatches.

Many fishermen confuse or misread the feeding behavior of fish. A disturbance on the surface of the stream is not always created by a trout plucking a mayfly dun or other insect from the surface of the water. Many times the fish's momentum in the pursuit of these nymphs or the close proximity of the insects to the surface causes the fish to break or disturb the water in the process of feeding on it. I can recall a number of instances over the years when I switched my fly selection from nymphs to adult imitations and failed to catch a thing because the fish were keying on emergent flies instead.

At the actual point of emergence—the time frame often referred to as the "final inch"—as the swimming or drifting nymph gets close to the surface, the wing case begins to split open down its center lengthwise and the folded wings of the adult fly begin to protrude first. The

wing case, which often has a silvery glisten to it, splits much like a plastic coin case when you squeeze it from the ends to open it. As the insect pushes against the water's surface tension, the friction against the husk of the nymphal skin allows the thoracic segment followed by the head of the adult to erupt from the casing. Once the adult's head and wings break free of the exoskeleton, it can extract its abdomen and tails quickly. This process can happen quickly in some species, while in others it's a much longer transformation and the emerging fly drifts for some time before finally freeing itself of the nymph's casing. Cool or rainy conditions often slow the hatching process and extend the duration of the emergence.

While hatching, many mayflies can become injured or suffer from some problem that prevents them from shedding the nymphal exoskeleton and hatching into an adult fly. Whether the problem results from an injury or from other conditions such as wind or turbulent water, a number of hatching flies become casualties as they struggle to free themselves of the surface tension or the shuck itself. Some hatching flies look as if they were capsized

Above: A pool on Little Pine Creek in north central Pennsylvania. Many feeding trout will focus on insects in the vulnerable transitional stages during a hatch. BARRY AND CATHY BECK

A nice brown trout taken with a Pale Sulphur Half-and-Half Emerger on Pennsylvania's Little Juniata River.

by a gust of wind or heavy currents and drift with one or both of their wings stuck in the surface film. Except for the spinner stage, at no other time is the insect in a more vulnerable position to feeding trout.

The history of flies designed to imitate emergent mayfly hatches is relatively new in terms of a sport as old as fly fishing. A solid argument can be made that many older patterns such as the British soft-hackled wet flies of W. C. Stewart and T. E. Pritt are taken by fish as imitations of emerging mayflies and caddis; however there is little documentation from these early writers that this relationship was by direct design on their part. In Pritt's *Yorkshire Trout Flies,* published in 1885, he briefly alludes to a relationship between his soft-hackled flies and the imitation of emerging insects. He writes, "It is far more difficult to imitate a perfect insect and to afterwards impart to it a semblance of life in or on the water, than it is to produce something which is sufficiently near a resemblance of an imperfectly developed insect, struggling to attain the surface of the stream."

Jim Leisenring introduces these same Yorkshire-style soft-hackle flies to American fishermen in his classic *The Art of Tying the Wet Fly*, published in 1941. Leisenring does not make any references to previously written material on the subject of the soft-hackled fly, but the influence of earlier British authors, particularly Pritt and Skues, is apparent in his work, and Leisenring's patterns feature many of the same materials and styles favored by these British writers, such as partridge, starling, grouse, woodcock, jackdaw, and plover hackles. Leisenring introduces a unique method for presenting his flies in a manner that would imitate the behavior of an emerging fly swimming toward the surface, a technique that would be called the Leisenring Lift. Leisenring sadly never expressed his thoughts on the correlation between his soft-hackle fly patterns and the emerging insects he was imitating in his own writings, but a second edition published in 1971 by his protégé Vernon Hidy assembled and explained Leisenring's theories behind the flies he crafted in an expanded version of the original manuscript.

All of these patterns are taken by fish subsurface or in the film as swimming or emerging flies, but the design of these soft-hackled wet flies is more suggestive rather than imitative. Fish keying on emergers often require patterns more specific and detailed in design if they are to be effective under these difficult stream conditions.

I prefer Z-Lon yarn fibers for tying emerger imitations. These fibers are triangular in cross section and reflect light better than fibers that are rounded or oval in cross section. Z-Lon is available in both a crinkly and a straight texture. Because Z-Lon does not absorb water, it is perfect for working on dry-fly wings. I use the crinkly variety for wings on the Yellow Stone, my Trico dun and spinner patterns, and the CDC Half-and-Half and Almost Dun emergers. JAY NICHOLS

Stalcup's Medallion Sheeting is a thin synthetic film that can be trimmed to any shape and creates realistic effects on mayfly, caddis, stonefly, and terrestrial patterns. Medallion Sheeting comes in an assortment of natural colors to match nearly any hatch you might encounter. I prefer to use this material for emerger patterns such as the Almost Dun series where I want a well-defined wing silhouette. JAY NICHOLS

Effective imitations of emerging flies have qualities of both the nymph and adult stages. Imitations need to not only look like this transitional stage, but they also must use materials that make a fly suspend both in the film of the stream surface and partially sunken below. Synthetic fibers such as Z-Lon and Darlon help to make emerger shucks translucent and sparkly, while thin synthetic films such as Shane Stalcup's Medallion Sheeting make it possible to construct realistic wings that are durable yet thin enough to cast well. CDC feathers not only help the fly float because of their unique physical properties but also create movement in the fly. Modern hooks like the Tiemco 206BL and Daiichi's 1120, 1130, and 1140 have curved shanks that do a great job of duplicating the arched posture of many emergent mayflies trying to extract themselves from the exoskeleton of the nymph stage.

Over the years I have experimented with a number of different emerger-type patterns and a variety of materials, making adjustments along the way to make them more effective. Two designs have worked out well in my own experiments on the stream: the Half-and-Half CDC Emerger and the Almost Dun.

The Half-and-Half is half nymph in appearance and half dun. The wing, tied as a post of CDC fibers, assists the angler in tracking the fly's drift, and the parachute hackle helps to imitate the legs of the dun, which have removed themselves from the nymph's exoskeleton, and also provide surface tension to suspend the fly in the film. I tie the abdomen on many of them from dark brown mottled turkey-tail fibers wrapped in the same manner as for a pheasant-tail nymph; the mottled black and brown is reminiscent of the color of many mayfly nymphs. For the trailing shucks on these emergers I prefer a sparse amount of crinkled Z-Lon yarn. Adding speckled or mottled fibers such as lemon wood duck or partridge to the shuck increases the realism.

The Almost Dun is a newer pattern that more closely imitates an almost completely emerged or crippled mayfly dun. In this pattern the dun is nearly free from the nymph's exoskeleton; the body of the dun is completely exposed and the wings are unfurled. A sparse collar of CDC fibers imitates the legs, adding some movement to the fly and improving floatation qualities. The Almost Dun does a great job of imitating a partially hatched dun and is effective especially over difficult fish in flat water. The well-defined wing profile tends to drift on one side or the other with one of the wings pressed against the surface of the water, which is common in many natural mayflies drifting on the surface.

TYING THE ALMOST DUN EMERGER (SULPHUR)

SULPHUR
(*Ephemerella dorothea dorothea* and *invaria*,
  ***Epeorus vitreus*)**

Hook:	#14–18 Daiichi 1130
Thread:	Light cahill 8/0 Uni-Thread
Shuck:	Three lemon wood-duck fibers and brown Z-Lon
Abdomen:	Sulphur Harrop Dry Fly Dubbing
Wing:	Light dun Medallion Sheeting
Hackle:	Sulphur CDC fibers tied as a collar
Thorax:	Same as abdomen

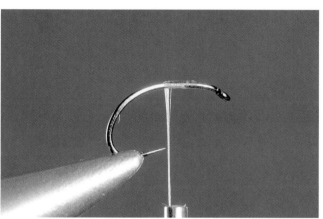

1. Clamp a curved light wire hook in the vise and attach 8/0 light cahill thread at the midpoint of the hook.

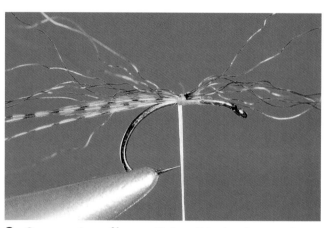

3. Cut a section of brown Z-Lon 2 inches long and separate 10 to 12 fibers to make the trailing shuck. Tie the fibers in at the same point as the wood duck.

2. Select three or four lemon wood-duck fibers. Tie in the wood-duck fibers at the midpoint. They should extend 2 to 2½ times the hook length. Trim the surplus.

4. Double the yarn back over the hook bend and wrap into place, working back to a point just above and beyond the end of the hook barb.

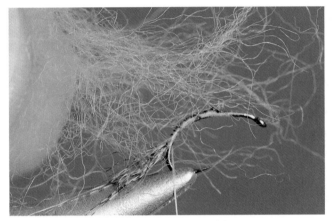

5. Trim the yarn shuck so that it is approximately the length of the hook shank.

6. Apply dubbing to the thread and begin wrapping it forward.

7. Create a tapered body, stopping three-fourths of the way to the hook eye. The forward end of the body should not taper off. A slight shoulder will help maintain separation in the wings when they are tied in.

8. Cut a 1-inch-long strip of light dun Medallion Sheeting as wide as the hook gap. Cut the sheeting lengthwise.

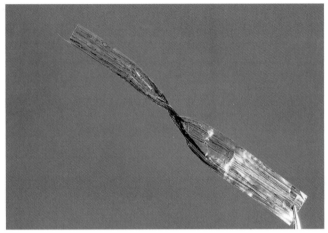

9. Grasp the strip near the center with both hands and twist it 180 degrees in the middle to create a pinched tie-in point in its center.

10. Tie the strip to the hook at its center with figure-eight turns of thread.

11. Fold the ends of the wing strip back so that they are at a 45-degree angle to the hook shank.

12. Take a few tight turns of thread over the wing bases to hold them in position.

13. The wing strips should now sit at a 45-degree angle to the abdomen of the fly.

14. Trim the wings to shape by first taking a vertical cut even with the end of the body. Cut both wings at the same time to keep them even.

15. The wings are cut to length. Note the angle of this first cut.

16. Next make a horizontal cut to establish the wing height.

17. The wing height should be 1½ times the gap of the hook. Use scissors to round off the corners if you wish.

20. Note how the trimmed feather tips make a more natural appearance than cutting them with scissors.

18. Select two full CDC feathers and stack them together with the tips of the feathers even. Cut a V in the tips of the feathers.

21. Straddle the fly with the CDC feathers from the front so that the tips of the fibers reach the hook bend and are evenly distributed on both sides of the fly.

19. Stroke the fibers tightly together and use your thumbnail against your index finger to even them out by breaking the tips of the CDC fibers.

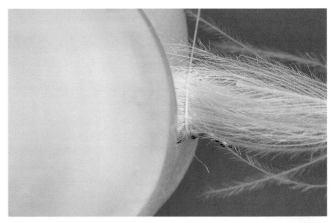

22. Grip the tips of the CDC fibers with your left thumb and forefinger so that the fibers are pinched tightly against the fly. Take one complete loose turn of thread around the CDC feathers, then apply tension with an upward pull to help distribute the fibers around the fly.

23. Take a few more tight turns of thread to anchor the CDC.

24. Trim off the butts.

25. Dub the remainder of the hook in front of the wings to create a head and thorax and whip-finish.

26. Trim the thread. The CDC fiber collar suspends the fly in the film and adds some movement, which is not common in many emerger or dry-fly patterns.

LIGHT OLIVE
(*Attenella attenuata, Drunella lata*)

Hook:	#12-16 Daiichi 1130
Thread:	Light olive 8/0 Uni-Thread
Shuck:	Three lemon wood-duck fibers and brown Z-Lon
Abdomen:	Pale olive and BWO Harrop Dry Fly Dubbing (50/50 mix)
Wing:	Medium dun Medallion Sheeting
Hackle:	Medium dun CDC fibers tied as a collar
Thorax:	Same as abdomen

BAETIS
(*Baetis* spp.)

Hook:	#18–22 Daiichi 1130
Thread:	Olive dun 8/0 Uni-Thread or olive 14/0 Sheer for smaller sizes
Shuck:	Three lemon wood-duck fibers and brown or olive Z-Lon
Abdomen:	BWO Harrop Dry Fly Dubbing
Wing:	Medium dun Medallion Sheeting
Hackle:	Olive CDC fibers tied as a collar
Thorax:	Same as abdomen

PALE SULPHUR
(*Ephemerella dorothea dorothea* and *invaria*, *Leucrocuta hebe*)

Hook:	#14–18 Daiichi 1130
Thread:	Light cahill 8/0 Uni-Thread
Shuck:	Three lemon wood-duck fibers and brown Z-Lon
Abdomen:	Pale yellow Harrop Dry Fly Dubbing
Wing:	Light dun Medallion Sheeting
Hackle:	Pale yellow CDC fibers tied as a collar
Thorax:	Same as abdomen

CREAM
(*Maccaffertium ithaca* and *modestum*, *Stenacron* spp.)

Hook:	#14–16 Daiichi 1130
Thread:	Light cahill 8/0 Uni-Thread
Shuck:	Three lemon wood-duck fibers and brown Z-Lon
Abdomen:	Light cahill Harrop Dry Fly Dubbing
Wing:	Clear Medallion Sheeting
Hackle:	Cream or natural tan CDC fibers tied as a collar
Thorax:	Same as abdomen

TAN
(*Maccaffertium vicarium*)

Hook:	#12-14 Daiichi 1130
Thread:	Tan 8/0 Uni-Thread
Shuck:	Three lemon wood-duck fibers and brown Z-Lon
Abdomen:	Dark tan Harrop Dry Fly Dubbing
Wing:	Mottled tan Medallion Sheeting
Hackle:	Natural tan CDC and brown partridge fibers tied as a collar
Thorax:	Same as abdomen

MAHOGANY
(*Ephemerella subvaria, Paraleptophlebia adoptiva* and *mollis*)

Hook:	#14-18 Daiichi 1130
Thread:	Wine 8/0 Uni-Thread
Shuck:	Three lemon wood-duck fibers and brown Z-Lon
Abdomen:	Mahogany Harrop Dry Fly Dubbing
Wing:	Light dun Medallion Sheeting
Hackle:	Natural dun CDC fibers tied as a collar
Thorax:	Same as abdomen

PINK MALE
(*Ephemerella subvaria*)

Hook:	#12-14 Daiichi 1130
Thread:	Tan 8/0 Uni-Thread
Shuck:	Three lemon wood-duck fibers and brown Z-Lon
Abdomen:	Hendrickson or Pink Albert Harrop Dry Fly Dubbing
Wing:	Dark dun Medallion Sheeting
Hackle:	Natural dark dun CDC fibers tied as a collar
Thorax:	Same as abdomen

ISONYCHIA
(*Isonychia bicolor*)

Hook:	#12 Daiichi 1130
Thread:	Dark brown or wine 8/0 Uni-Thread
Shuck:	Dark brown Z-Lon
Abdomen:	One-third mahogany, ⅔ Trico Harrop Dry Fly Dubbing
Wing:	Medium dun Medallion Sheeting
Hackle:	Natural dark dun CDC fibers tied as a collar
Thorax:	Same as abdomen

TRICO
(*Tricorythodes* spp.)

Hook:	#22-24 Daiichi 1130
Thread:	Black 8/0 Uni-Thread
Shuck:	Black Z-Lon
Abdomen:	Black Superfine dubbing
Wing:	Clear Medallion Sheeting
Hackle:	Black CDC fibers tied as a collar
Thorax:	Same as abdomen

TYING THE HALF-AND-HALF CDC EMERGER (MAHOGANY)

MAHOGANY
(*Ephemerella subvaria, Paraleptophlebia adoptiva*
and *mollis*)

Hook:	#14–18 Daiichi 1130
Thread:	Wine 8/0 Uni-Thread
Shuck:	Three lemon wood–duck fibers and brown Z-Lon
Abdomen:	Dark brown mottled turkey-tail fibers
Rib:	Fine gold wire
Thorax:	Mahogany Harrop Dry Fly Dubbing
Wing:	Natural dun CDC
Hackle (optional):	Medium or bronze dun

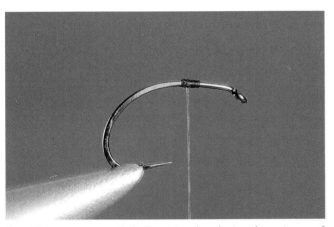

1. Clamp a curved light-wire hook in the vise and attach wine 8/0 thread at the midpoint of the hook.

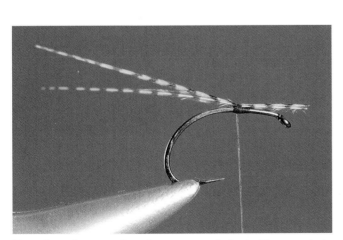

2. Select three or four lemon wood–duck fibers and tie them in at the midpoint of the hook. The fibers should extend 2 to 2½ times the length of the hook shank. Trim off the butts.

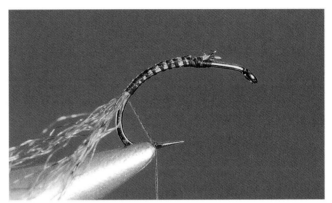

3. Cut a section of brown Z-Lon approximately 2 inches long and separate 8 to 10 fibers. Tie these in at their midpoint at the center of the hook shank. Pull the ends of the yarn fibers back and wrap back one-third of the way around the hook bend, binding the tails and shuck down on top of the hook as you go.

4. Trim the yarn fibers to equal the length of the hook shank. From a dark brown mottled turkey tail select three or four fibers. Trim the first half-inch from their tips and bind them to the hook at their base.

5. Wrap the tying thread forward ⅛ inch and tie in a length of fine gold wire on the underside of the hook. Wrap back to the base of the shuck to secure the wire.

6. Wrap the tying thread forward two-thirds the distance to the hook eye.

7. Wrap the turkey-tail fibers forward, stopping when you reach the tying thread. Tie off the turkey fibers with a few turns of thread and trim off the fiber butts.

8. Wrap the ribbing wire forward in even turns to create segmentation and reinforce the abdomen. Tie off the ribbing wire and break it off. Wrap the thread forward so that it is at the center of the remaining unused hook shank. Select two full natural dun CDC feathers and stack them together with the tips even.

9. Tie in the CDC feathers on top of the hook shank with the tips extending past the hook eye. The wings should be equal to 1½ times the hook gap. Trim off the butts of the CDC feathers.

10. Pull the CDC fibers into an upright position and take a few turns of thread in front of them.

11. Take turns of thread around the base of the CDC fibers to post the wing, wrapping up ¹⁄₁₆ inch, then back down to the hook shank.

12. Wrap the tying thread back to the end of the abdomen.

13. Apply dubbing to the thread and wrap a thorax, stopping at the base of the wings. Select a natural dun or bronze dun hackle and remove the webby fibers from the base. Tie in the hackle by the stem with the glossy side up, making sure to leave ¹⁄₈ inch of bare hackle stem exposed.

14. Take one open turn of the hackle up the wing post.

15. Wrap down the post in close turns.

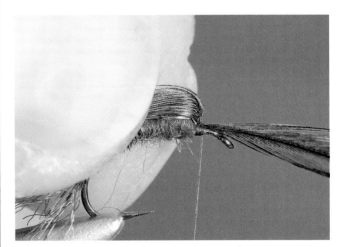

16. Hold the hackle fibers back out of the way and tie off the hackle tip on the hook shank immediately in front of the wings. Trim off the tip of the hackle.

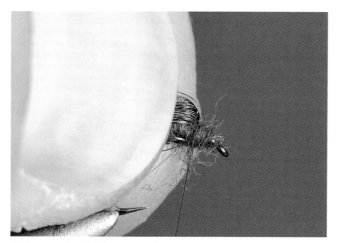

17. Apply dubbing to the thread and build the front section of the thorax.

18. End the thorax with enough room to whip-finish.

19. This realistic imitation of a partially emerged mayfly has characteristics of both the nymph and dun stages. The parachute hackle and CDC wing post permit the fly to sit suspended in the film like the natural and make it visible to both fish and fishermen.

LIGHT OLIVE
(*Attenella attenuata, Drunella lata*)

Hook:	#12-16 Daiichi 1130
Thread:	Light olive 8/0 Uni-Thread
Shuck:	Three lemon wood-duck fibers and brown Z-Lon
Abdomen:	Dark brown mottled turkey-tail fibers
Rib:	Fine gold wire
Thorax:	Golden olive Superfine dubbing
Wing:	Natural dun CDC
Hackle (optional):	Grizzly dyed light olive

BAETIS
(*Baetis* spp.)

Hook:	#18-20 Daichii 1130
Thread:	Olive dun 8/0 Uni-Thread or olive 14/0 Sheer for smaller sizes
Tails:	Three lemon wood-duck fibers and/or Baetis olive Z-Lon
Abdomen:	Dark brown turkey-tail fibers
Rib:	Fine gold wire
Thorax:	Olive Superfine dubbing
Wings:	Natural dun CDC
Hackle:	Grizzly dyed golden olive

SULPHUR
(*Ephemerella dorothea dorothea* and *invaria*, *Epeorus vitreus*)

Hook:	#14-18 Daiichi 1130
Thread:	Light cahill 8/0 Uni-Thread
Shuck:	Three lemon wood-duck fibers and brown Z-Lon
Abdomen:	Dark brown mottled turkey-tail fibers
Rib:	Fine gold wire
Thorax:	Sulphur Harrop Dry Fly Dubbing
Wing:	Dyed light dun CDC
Hackle (optional):	Cream-dyed pastel orange or light ginger

PALE SULPHUR
(*Ephemerella dorothea dorothea* and *invaria*, *Leucrocuta hebe*)

Hook:	#14-18 Daiichi 1130
Thread:	Light cahill 8/0 Uni-Thread
Shuck:	Three lemon wood-duck fibers and brown Z-Lon
Abdomen:	Dark brown mottled turkey-tail fibers
Rib:	Fine gold wire
Thorax:	Sulphur yellow Superfine dubbing
Wing:	Dyed light dun CDC
Hackle (optional):	Cream-dyed pastel orange or light ginger

TAN
(*Maccaffertium vicarium*)

Hook: #12-14 Daiichi 1130
Thread: Tan 8/0 Uni-Thread
Shuck: Three pheasant-tail fibers and brown Z-Lon
Abdomen: Dark brown mottled turkey-tail fibers
Rib: Fine gold wire
Thorax: Tan Superfine dubbing
Wing: Natural tan CDC
Hackle (optional): Cree or barred ginger

PINK MALE
(*Ephemerella subvaria*)

Hook: #12-14 Daiichi 1130
Thread: Tan 8/0 Uni-Thread
Shuck: Three lemon wood-duck fibers and brown Z-Lon
Abdomen: Dark brown mottled turkey-tail fibers
Rib: Fine gold wire
Thorax: Hendrickson or Pink Albert Harrop Dry Fly Dubbing
Wing: Natural dark dun CDC
Hackle (optional): Medium or bronze dun

ISONYCHIA
(*Isonychia bicolor*)

Hook: #12 Daiichi 1130
Thread: Wine 8/0 Uni-Thread
Shuck: Dark brown Z-Lon
Abdomen: Dark brown mottled turkey-tail fibers
Rib: Fine gold wire
Thorax: Mix of 1/3 mahogany, 2/3 Trico Harrop Dry Fly Dubbing
Wing: Natural dark dun CDC
Hackle: Medium or bronze dun

4

The Baetis Olive Hatch

The Baetis species are without question of paramount importance to the angler, as they represent a valuable year-round food source for the trout.

AL CAUCCI AND BOB NASTASI, *HATCHES*

One trait that separates the species of the genus *Baetis* from other mayflies is that they are truly multibrooded, and hatches occur several times during the year. In the East they are often the first mayflies to hatch each year, making their first appearance beginning in March, followed by a second brood that begins to emerge in September but can often continue through October depending on temperatures. This is often the final mayfly hatch of the season, making them both the "Alpha and the Omega" of the hatch season, the begin-

ning and the end. On some of the limestone streams where water temperatures can remain relatively consistent throughout the year, the *Baetis* Olives can hatch almost year-round, and I always carry a good selection of them in my vest as hatches can be unpredictable.

The *Baetis* nymphs are of the swimming variety, moving in short bursts, and can often be found in good populations in the calmer sections of the stream among the gravel and vegetation rather than in the faster reaches of water. The nymphs average 4 to 9 millimeters in length,

Baetis *hatches are often the first mayfly hatches of the year, with the first broods emerging in March. This stream is Mud Run in the Pocono Mountains of northeast Pennsylvania.* EMILY RAMSAY

What's in a Name?

The tiny mayflies of the Baetidae family are commonly referred to by many fishermen as "Blue-Winged Olives" although most of the species in this category neither are olive in color nor have blue wings. The nickname Blue-Winged Olive (BWO) is also used for many other mayflies with olive-tinted bodies such as *Attenella attenuata* and *Drunella lata*, which are classified in separate mayfly families, as well as a lengthy list of others within the Baetidae family. Confusion often reigns among anglers when these mayflies come up in conversation. Which species are you referring to when you say Blue-Winged Olive? All of the mayflies commonly referred to as Olives or BWOs enjoy widely different characteristics, coloration, sizes, emergence periods, and habitats. At times it does seem to be trivial or even worse to worry about some of the minute details of mayfly identification, but it is often helpful to have a fundamental knowledge of mayfly entomology to better understand the insects we hope to imitate with our flies. While it may seem unimportant to many fishermen to have the ability to identify these flies down to the species level, it is important to have a good basic knowledge of the various mayflies and their behaviors and habits to be better prepared on the stream.

Within the Baetidae family is a long list of individual genuses, including *Acentrella*, *Acerpenna*, *Callibaetis*, *Centroptilum*, *Cloeon*, *Pseudocloeon*, and *Baetis*, among others. Nearly all the genuses represented here share similar olive-toned coloration with the exception of the gray-speckled *Callibaetis*. All of these small olive-colored mayflies grouped collectively within the Baetidae family make mayfly discussions difficult at best, and entomologists seem to compound the problem by continually renaming, reclassifying, and regrouping this collection of mayflies—making it almost impossible to stay current. The mayfly species for this chapter are important members of the *Baetis* genus, which comprises, among others, *B. tricaudatus*, *intercalaris*, *flavistriga*, *brunneicolor*, and *bicaudatus*. To minimize the confusion created by using a looser and broader term like Blue-Winged Olives, I call them "*Baetis* Olives."

and the hook sizes I most commonly use to match them are from 18 to 22. The nymphs are streamlined and heavily ringed in their abdomens with fine gill plates that are arranged nearly perpendicular to the segments of the body, making a turkey biot a nearly perfect imitation of this feature when wrapped so that the fuzzy leading edge of the biot is oriented toward the tail of the fly. As the biot fiber is wrapped forward the flue creates a raised rib that simulates both the body segmentation and the illusion of gills. The tails consist of three fibers with the outside fibers being slightly longer than the center tail. The thorax is robust with an oversize wing case that is heavily notched and much darker in color than the rest of the nymph. When viewed from the side the nymph's thorax appears to have a dramatic humplike profile. The nymph pattern presented here uses Thin Skin vinyl sheeting trimmed to create this deeply notched wing case, which is then coated with five-minute epoxy to nicely duplicate the raised hump profile of the thoracic section. The legs of the nymphs are thin and fairly long and are a light olive color, mottled with darker markings. At rest the legs are spread to the sides, and they are tucked back under the thorax when the nymph swims. The legs are well imitated with a speckled Hungarian partridge hackle dyed a light shade of olive. Most of us use up the brown tinted feathers on a partridge skin and eventually find a number of gray feathers remaining on the skin that have limited application in many fly patterns. I dye these remaining feathers in a number of colors to extend their usefulness.

The Baetis Nymph is a great addition to your fly boxes. It was successful on the Missouri River in Montana this past season and works well tied traditionally or with a bead head. The small nymphs are an important food item and are available to the trout year-round, making the nymph an effective pattern anytime of the year on streams with good populations of them. In the days preceding an emergence, the nymphs become active and often move toward shallow waters or will climb things such as vegetation to get closer to the stream's surface.

At the surface the drifting nymphs begin hatching and will drift for some time before emerging as duns. The species of the genus *Baetis* show a preference for hatching on overcast, drizzly days, and some of the best fishing takes place on the rainy days that chase most fishermen off the stream. Cooler, wet weather always seems to bring a higher level of difficulty for flies to hatch as quickly as they will under warmer, less humid conditions, and the *Baetis* species struggle with these issues. As a result, an emerger or a cripple-type pattern can be effective fished in the film, and a good selection of patterns

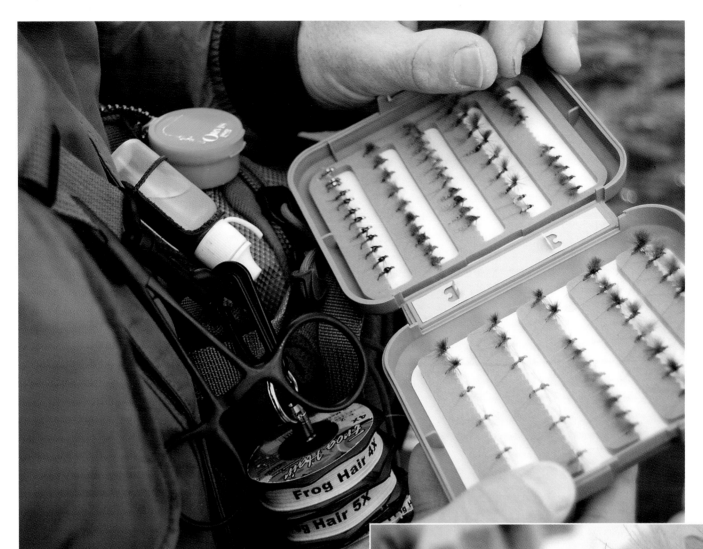

Always carry a good assortment of Baetis Olive *patterns on the stream. These multibrooded mayflies can hatch a number of times during the year, particularly in the early spring and later in the fall.* WES OSBORNE

can be important to success as fish may show a stronger preference for this in-between phase of the hatch. Two emerger patterns presented in this book, the Half-and-Half Emerger and the Almost Dun, are effective imitations of this important stage of transitional flies and crippled duns, and both patterns have worked well for me when trout show a preference for this stage of the hatch. Another favorite *Baetis* emerger of mine is based on Shane Stalcup's Loop Wing Emerger series, which I tie to be more species specific to imitate these flies. The loop wing pattern closely resembles the period when the nymph has reached the surface and is just beginning the process of emerging from the nymphal exoskeleton.

Although many of the duns are varying shades of tan or brown with overtones of olive, many of these flies can be shades of cinnamon to reddish brown. The range of

The author's fly box contains several versions of emerger patterns including cripples, all of which can be useful depending on conditions. JAY NICHOLS

An immature Baetis *nymph. The pale color of the wing cases indicates that the nymph is not ready to hatch. Use this clue when examining nymphs on the stream.*

Below: An example of a lighter colored Baetis *dun. Because* Baetis *species range in color from light to dark shades of olive, carry several patterns to match them.*

A Baetis *nymph that is fully mature and ready to emerge. The nymph's well-defined segmentation makes a turkey biot a great way to imitate the row of gill plates on each side of the abdomen.*

Above: An example of a darker colored Baetidae *family dun. Note that this female dun lacks hind wings, a common trait of many mayflies in this family; others may have dwarfed hind wings.*

A fully mature Acentrella *nymph that is ready to hatch. Note that the wing cases are very dark, nearly black, at this stage and notched. A material like Thin Skin coated with epoxy creates this effect in nymph imitations.*

A nice brown about to be released. Many larger fish focus on the little nymphs swimming to the surface during the Baetis *hatch.*
BARRY AND CATHY BECK

color variation in the *Baetis* species makes it important to capture and inspect a specimen before attempting to match them. A small aquarium net is an invaluable tool to carry for capturing specimens in the air or in the water and works better than trying to capture an insect with your hands or hat. The duns of the *Baetis* species group can be easily identified from the other olive-tinted mayflies by examining their hind wings, which can be dwarfed in size or be completely absent. The hind wing set is small when present and is not readily visible until you look closely. Other members of the olive mayfly category such as *Attenella attenuata*, *Drunella lata*, and *D. cornutella* have much larger, well-developed hind wings consistent with many other species such as those of the genuses *Isonychia*, *Anthopotamus*, *Maccaffertium*, and *Ephemera*. The legs of most of the *Baetis* duns are an olive or golden olive color, and I prefer to use a dyed grizzly hackle to match them more accurately.

The small duns will often drift for extended lengths of time and distance before finally gaining the air and heading for streamside vegetation. As a result the trout have the opportunity to take them at their leisure, which is often characterized by a higher level of selectivity when combined with the relatively calm water that the flies prefer. The water often has numerous flies drifting on the surface, and the trout take them with calm riseforms. I carry two basic patterns to imitate the dun stage: the CDC Thorax Dun, which uses a hackle palmered in open turns over the thorax and trimmed flush on the underside, and a CDC Comparadun, which uses no hackle and presents a more defined silhouette of the wings for more demanding conditions. I dress each pattern style in several colors to match the naturals I encounter on the stream.

The final stage of the *Baetis* hatch, the spinner (imago), presents another challenge for the angler. The spinner is not nearly as important as the dun stage because only the

A calm pool on Pennsylvania's Kettle Creek offers good habitat for Baetis Olives *and a great opportunity to fish their hatches.* Baetis Olives *are common on many streams.* BARRY AND CATHY BECK

males usually fall to the water spent. The females in most of the *Baetis* species do not drop to the surface as spent spinners, but instead dive underwater to lay their eggs. Many females will land on trees or rocks sticking out of the water and crawl down them to lay their eggs on the stream bottom. After depositing their eggs the females will drift in the current as they try to reach the surface again, presenting easy targets for trout. A small olive-toned wet fly or soft-hackled pattern or even a sunken spinner pattern can be effective when fished dead drift to imitate this activity. At times, spinnerfalls can bring good numbers of fish to the surface and provide challenging fishing.

TYING THE BAETIS NYMPH

BAETIS NYMPH

Hook: #18-20 Daichii 1560
Thread: Olive dun 8/0 Uni-Thread
Bead (optional): 1/16-inch gold or olive
Tails: Hungarian partridge dyed light olive
Body: Olive turkey biot
Thorax: Olive Australian opossum
Wing Case: Black Thin Skin notched and coated with five-minute epoxy
Legs: Hungarian partridge dyed light olive (V-notch)

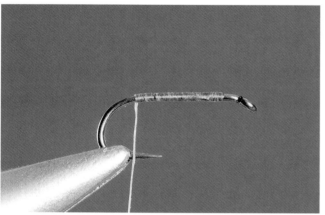

1. Clamp a 1XL nymph hook in the vise, attaching 8/0 olive dun thread behind the hook eye. Wrap the tying thread back toward the bend to create a thread base, stopping at a point over the end of the hook barb.

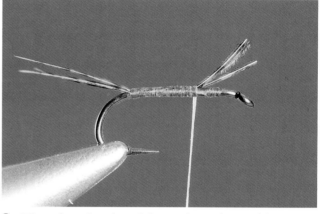

3. Wrap the tying thread forward just short of the eye to secure the butts of the tail fibers and level the thread base. Trim the butt ends.

2. Select three partridge-hackle fibers dyed light olive and tie them in on top of the hook shank. The tails should be equal in length to the hook shank. Take a turn of thread underneath the tails to separate them and add a drop of head cement to the bases.

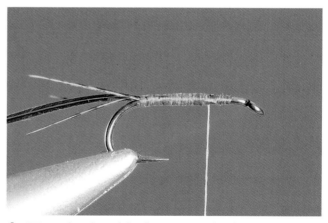

4. Wrap the thread back again to the base of the tails and tie in an olive-dyed turkey biot by its tip. Orient the biot so that it is flat on top of the hook shank and the raised edge is pointed away from you.

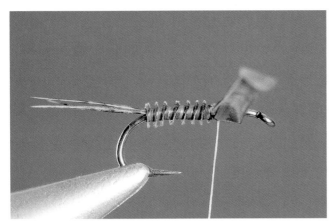

5. Grip the base of the biot with your hackle pliers and pull it upward and perpendicular to the hook shank. The raised edge should now be to the left side. Wrap the biot forward in close turns, stopping two-thirds of the way to the hook eye.

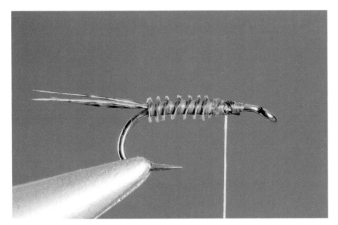

6. Trim off the excess biot fiber closely.

7. Dub a thorax of olive Australian opossum that is twice the thickness of the abdomen and tapers toward the hook eye.

8. Select a Hungarian partridge hackle and cut a V notch in the tip of the feather. Stroke back the fibers at the base of the feather to leave 8 to 10 fibers remaining on each side of the stem. Straddle the thorax with the prepared hackle. It should be flat on top of the fly with the tips extending half the length of the hook shank. Pinch the fibers against the sides of the thorax with your left thumb and forefinger to hold them in place. Take one loose turn around the feather before pulling it tight. Continue to hold the fibers in place and take several more firm turns of thread to secure. The legs should lie back on the sides of the thorax. Trim off the surplus hackle.

9. Cut a strip of black Thin Skin the same width as the hook gap. Remove the paper backing and fold the tip of the strip lengthwise. Use fingernail clippers to cut a notch in the tip of the strip.

10. Hold the prepared strip flat on top of the thorax so that the notch of the wing case comes to the end of the thorax dubbing. Tie down the wing case with firm turns of thread. Build a small head from tying thread. Whip-finish, trim off the thread, and apply head cement.

11. Coat the wing case with five-minute epoxy. The well-defined segmentation of the abdomen and the deep notch in the wing case are both predominant features of the natural nymph.

TYING THE BAETIS LOOPWING EMERGER

BAETIS LOOPWING EMERGER

Hook:	#18-20 Daichii 1130
Thread:	Olive dun 8/0 Uni-Thread or olive 14/0 Sheer for smaller sizes
Tails:	Hungarian partridge dyed light olive and olive brown Z-Lon or Blue Ribbon Baetis olive
Body:	Olive Superfine dubbing
Thorax:	Olive Superfine dubbing
Wing Bud:	Natural dun CDC
Legs:	Hungarian partridge dyed light olive
Head:	Olive Superfine dubbing

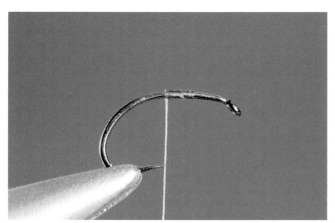

1. Clamp a light-wire curved nymph hook in the vise. Attach olive dun 8/0 thread at the midpoint. Use 14/0 thread for the smallest sizes.

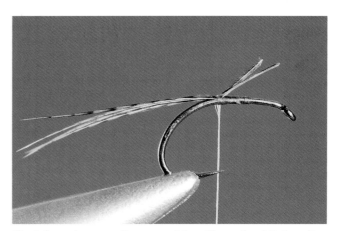

2. Select three or four partridge fibers dyed light olive and tie them in at the midpoint. The fibers should extend twice the length of the hook shank.

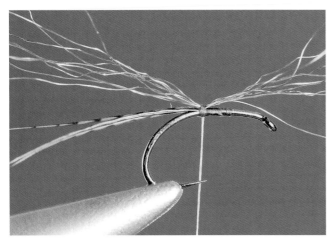

3. Cut a section of olive brown Z-Lon an inch long and separate 8 to 10 fibers to make the trailing shuck. Tie the fibers in by their center at the midpoint of the hook.

4. Fold the Z-Lon fibers back and wrap the thread back toward the bend, securing the tail and shuck fibers, and stop at a point just above and beyond the end of the hook barb. Trim the trailing shuck to length, making it approximately the length of the hook shank.

5. Apply olive Superfine dubbing to the thread and build a tapered body for half the hook length.

6. Select a very full natural dun CDC feather and tie it in by the tips. The feather should be on top of the hook shank and extend back past the tails. Use two feathers if needed.

7. Trim off the excess tips of the CDC feathers.

8. Apply olive Superfine dubbing and build a full thorax. The thorax should taper toward the hook eye and stop well short of it.

9. Select a partridge hackle dyed light olive and cut a V notch in the tip to remove the center stem. Stroke back the base fibers so that 8 or 10 fibers remain on each side of the feather. Straddle the thorax with the feather held flat and the fibers extending two-thirds of the way to the hook bend. Pinch the partridge hackle fibers tight against the sides of the thorax with your left thumb and forefinger to hold them in place. Take a loose turn of tying thread around the feather before pulling tight. While holding the feather in position take several more firm turns to secure it and trim off the excess partridge feather.

10. Fold the CDC feathers forward toward the hook eye and push them back a short distance to create an open loop of CDC fibers. Tie the feathers tightly on top of the hook shank.

11. Trim off the surplus CDC feathers closely.

12. Dub a small head of olive Superfine dubbing, whip-finish, and cut off the thread. Loopwing-style emergers sit in the film of the water with the tail and trailing shuck submerged, making an accurate profile of a dun trying to shed the nymphal husk. It is important to keep the CDC loop open so that it captures air and helps the fly float well.

BAETIS HALF-AND-HALF EMERGER

Hook: #18-20 Daichii 1130
Thread: Olive dun 8/0 Uni-Thread or olive 14/0 Sheer for smaller sizes
Tails: Three lemon wood-duck fibers and olive brown Z-Lon
Body: Dark brown turkey-tail fibers wrapped and ribbed with fine gold wire
Thorax: Olive Superfine dubbing
Wings: Natural dun CDC post
Hackle: Grizzly dyed golden olive

BAETIS ALMOST DUN EMERGER

Hook: #18-22 Daiichi 1130
Thread: Olive dun 8/0 Uni-Thread or olive 14/0 Sheer for smaller sizes
Shuck: Three lemon wood-duck fibers and brown Z-Lon
Abdomen: BWO Harrop Dry Fly Dubbing
Wing: Medium dun Medallion Sheeting
Hackle: Olive CDC fibers tied as a collar
Thorax: Same as abdomen

BAETIS CDC COMPARADUN (Dark)

Hook: #18-22 Daichii 1180
Thread: Olive dun 8/0 Uni-Thread or olive 14/0 Sheer for smaller sizes
Tails: Four dark dun Microfibetts
Body: BWO Superfine dubbing
Wings: Natural dun CDC
Head: BWO Superfine dubbing

BAETIS CDC COMPARADUN (Light)

Hook:	#18-22 Daichii 1180
Thread:	Olive dun 8/0 Uni-Thread or olive 14/0 Sheer for smaller sizes
Tails:	Four dark dun Microfibetts
Body:	Olive Superfine dubbing
Wings:	Natural dun CDC
Head:	Olive Superfine dubbing

BAETIS CDC THORAX DUN (Dark)

Hook:	#18-22 Daichii 1180
Thread:	Olive dun 8/0 Uni-Thread or olive 14/0 Sheer for smaller sizes
Tails:	Four olive Microfibetts
Body:	BWO turkey or goose biot
Thorax:	BWO Superfine dubbing
Wings:	Natural dun CDC
Hackle:	Grizzly dyed golden olive

BAETIS CDC THORAX DUN (Light)

Hook:	#18-22 Daichii 1180
Thread:	Olive dun 8/0 Uni-Thread or olive 14/0 Sheer for smaller sizes
Tails:	Four olive Microfibetts
Body:	Olive turkey or goose biot
Thorax:	Olive Superfine dubbing
Wings:	Natural dun CDC
Hackle:	Grizzly dyed golden olive

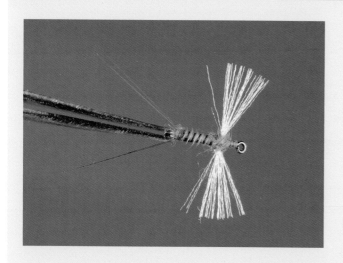

BAETIS DNA SPINNER

Hook: #18-22 Daichii 1180
Thread: Cinnamon 14/0 Sheer
Tails: Dark dun Microfibetts
Body: BWO turkey or goose biot
Thorax: Brown olive Superfine dubbing
Wings: Shrimp DNA Frosty Fish Fiber

SUBMERGED BAETIS SPINNER

Bead: Cyclops or tungsten
Hook: #18-22 Daichii 1180
Thread: Olive dun 8/0 Uni-Thread or olive
               14/0 Sheer for smaller sizes
Tails: Three dark dun Microfibetts
Body: BWO turkey or goose biot
Thorax: Brown-olive Australian opossum
Legs: Hungarian partridge dyed light olive
Wings: Clear Medallion Sheeting
Head: Brown-olive Australian opossum

5

The Sulphur Hatch

This hatch provides some of the most pleasant fishing of the entire season.

DOUG SWISHER AND CARL RICHARDS, *SELECTIVE TROUT*

Sulphurs arrive in May and hatch in abundant numbers through June when the weather is pleasant and the water levels more predictable and stable than earlier in the season. Sulphurs are important to fish at all parts of the insect's life cycle, including the transitional stages of their emergence. Multiple stages of the hatch may be active at the same time. To be successful under these challenging conditions, observant anglers must determine which specific stage of the hatch trout are keying on and have a good selection of flies to imitate each of them.

Many anglers use the name "Sulphur" to describe any mayfly with a yellowish overall color such as *Epeorus vitreus*, various *Stenacron* species, *Anthopotamus distinctus*, *Ephemerella invaria*, and *E. dorothea dorothea*. All of these mayfly duns, however, have different biologies, behaviors, and emergence traits worth considering. In this chapter, the mayfly species I discuss is *E. dorothea dorothea*,

A group of Sulphurs (Ephemerella invaria). Sulphurs are an important hatch on many eastern streams.
BARRY AND CATHY BECK

Sulphur fishing on Pennsylvania's Little Juniata River near Barree. The Little J is famous for its Sulphur hatches.
BARRY AND CATHY BECK

commonly called the Little Sulphur, and a closely related mayfly species *E. invaria*, which is commonly called the Big Sulphur. Both hatches are similar at all stages of their life cycles and occur on the same watersheds. From an imitative standpoint they can be treated as the same insect.

The key difference between the two mayfly species is the size of the insects and their emergence periods. *E. invaria* (#14-16) typically hatches in the earlier part of May in the evenings whereas the smaller *E. dorothea* (#16-18) follows later in the month of May and often hatches well into June. On some streams, Sulphurs can hatch well into the summer months. The West Branch of the Delaware has good summertime emergences. *E. invaria* and *dorothea* duns are nearly identical in color, and I use the same fly patterns in different sizes to imitate both species.

The small, dark crawling nymphs are poorly suited to living in faster water and lack the ability to swim rapidly. They will often drift for considerable distances before finally emerging, which makes nymph imitations important when fishing the hatch. When the nymphs finally reach the water's surface, the winged duns often drift for

long periods while trying to shed their nymphal skin, many becoming damaged or crippled during this time. Because many trout seem to favor feeding on this more vulnerable in-between stage of the hatch, emerger patterns are essential to successful fishing. I prefer patterns tied with CDC, which traps and holds air in its fibers, to keep the fly in the film and make it move realistically. Another effective emerger pattern I use, based on one of Shane Stalcup's designs, features wings made from Medallion Sheeting and a collar of CDC. Many of the historic English wet flies that were tied to imitate the "Pale Wateries," such as the Tup's Indispensable, the Partridge and Yellow, and the Little Marryatt, are also excellent and effective imitations of the emerging Sulphurs here in North America.

The duns often only begin to hatch in the last 30 minutes of the evening just before dark, which makes it difficult to see and track the drift of a fly, despite its light overall color. Overcast conditions, however, can trigger fly hatches earlier in the day. The duns frequently hatch in the calmer stretches of a stream where the trout can clearly scrutinize imitations and take their time feeding in the slower currents. The duns may drift for long

*A female Sulphur spinner (*Ephemerella dorothea dorothea*).*

*Below: The Sulphur nymph, a crawling variety that has a robust thorax and head and very thin legs, usually occupies calmer currents. Pictured is a Big Sulphur nymph (*Ephemerella invaria*).*

*A female Sulphur dun (*Ephemerella invaria*).* JAY NICHOLS

distances as they dry their wings before flight, making them an easy-to-capture meal for the trout. Because of the slower currents on these glassy pools, trout will often reject a drifting dun or emerger imitation if they detect the slightest drag in the fly's drift.

From stream to stream—depending on the water chemistry—Sulphurs can vary from a pale primrose yellow or pale yellow with olive highlights to a light reddish orange. In some watersheds the duns will often have a pale yellow abdomen and a light orange thorax. Trout often become selective to the body and thorax colors of the naturals, and I carry different shades to match the insects on the streams I frequent. The wings can vary from a light yellowish tint to varying shades of light blue dun. The legs are usually nearly the same color as the fly's body; on patterns such as thorax-type duns, I use the hackle from a cape dyed a pale pastel orange or honey dun. Effective imitations also need to mimic the light

pattern of the natural mayfly and must sit flush on the surface. I favor a thorax-style dun with hackle fibers trimmed flush on the underside of the fly or a CDC Comparadun-style pattern. High-floating patterns with hackles wrapped in the traditional manner to keep the fly's body and thorax portions off the surface often fail under difficult flat-water conditions.

Mating swarms of spinners appear over the water just before dark, and I have many fond memories of fishing spinnerfalls. Most mayfly spinners deposit their eggs in the water by dipping the surface multiple times and then falling spent on the surface. The Sulphur spinners can often fall on the surface with intact egg sacs, and some anglers incorporate this into their imitations using a light orange or yellow dubbing ball to separate the tail fibers. Like the dun stage, there can also be variation in color between different watersheds, so I carry both a light and a darker spinner pattern in my fly box.

TYING THE SULPHUR NYMPH

SULPHUR NYMPH

Hook:	#14-18 Daiichi 1560
Thread:	Camel 8/0 Uni-Thread
Tails:	Three dark wood-duck fibers
Abdomen:	Dark brown mottled turkey-tail fibers
Gills:	Tan marabou fibers
Rib:	Fine gold wire
Thorax:	Bleached ginger SLF Squirrel Dubbing
Wing Case:	Mottled oak Thin Skin coated with five-minute epoxy
Legs:	Brown partridge hackle

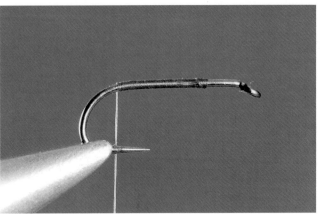

1. Clamp a 1XL nymph hook in the vise and attach the thread at the midpoint. Wrap the tying thread toward the hook bend, stopping at a point over the end of the barb.

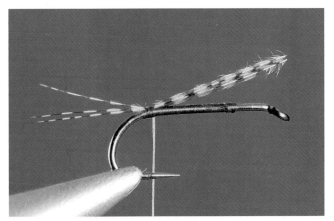

2. Select and tie in three well-marked lemon wood-duck flank fibers so that the tails are slightly shorter than the length of the hook shank. Be sure to keep the fibers on top of the hook shank.

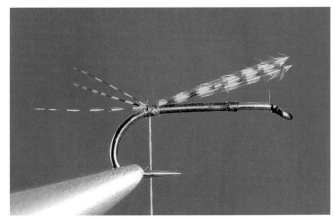

3. Take a turn of thread under the tail fibers to lift and spread them. Take a turn of thread between each tail fiber to maintain separation and add a tiny drop of head cement at the base.

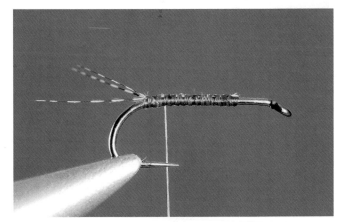

4. Trim the butts of the tailing fibers closely and advance the tying thread forward to a point even with the hook point.

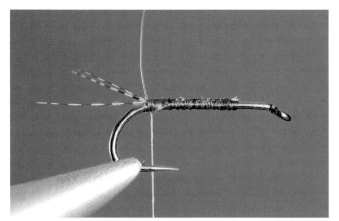

5. Attach a length of fine gold wire on the underside of the hook shank, wrapping back to the base of the tails.

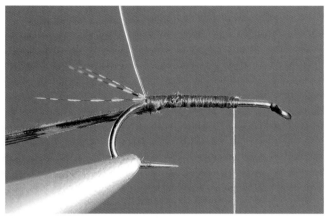

6. Select three or four dark brown mottled turkey-tail fibers and trim off the first half inch of the tips. Bind the fibers by the tips and advance the thread forward three-fourths of the way to the hook eye.

7. Wind the turkey-tail fibers forward for two-thirds of the hook shank and tie them off. Trim the butts of the turkey tail closely.

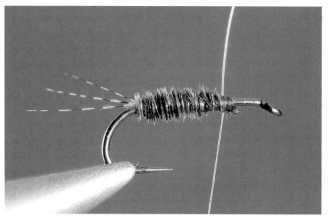

8. Wind the ribbing wire forward in evenly spaced turns over the length of the body. Tie off the wire and break it off.

9. Advance the tying thread to the hook eye.

10. Cut a strip of Thin Skin slightly narrower than the hook gap and tie it in at the eye. The strip should be pointing forward over the hook eye with the shiny side facing upward. Hold the strip flat on top of the hook eye and take one loose turn of thread around it. Pull the thread tight to pinch down the width of the strip and anchor it in place. Trim off the butt of the strip if necessary and take a few more turns of thread. Wrap the thread back to the end of the body.

11. Select a tan marabou feather and cut a notch in its tip, removing the center quill. Preen the fibers together, and using your thumbnail against your forefinger, break off the tips of the marabou fibers to even them in length.

12. Straddle the hook with the prepared marabou feather so that the fibers extend to the midpoint of the body. Pinch the marabou against the sides of the abdomen with your left thumb and forefinger and take a full turn of thread around the feather before pulling the thread taut.

13. Take several more turns of the thread to secure and trim the butts of the feather. The marabou fibers should be close along the sides of the body.

14. Build a thorax from bleached squirrel dubbing. The thorax should be twice the diameter of the abdomen.

15. Select a well-marked brown partridge hackle and cut a notch in the tip. Stroke back the feather fibers from the base so that only 8 or 10 fibers remain on each side of the stem. Hold the prepared hackle so that it straddles the thorax with the fibers extending approximately half the length of the fly and pinch the fibers against the thorax with your left thumb and forefinger. Take a loose turn of thread around the partridge hackle and pull the thread tight. Take several more turns of thread to secure and trim the hackle butts.

16. Build a head of bleached squirrel dubbing the same diameter as the thorax. The tying thread should be behind the head.

17. Pull the Thin Skin strip back over the head and thorax tightly and bind it in place to form a small head.

18. Whip-finish and trim the thread. Cut the Thin Skin to form a wing case that is half the length of the abdomen/thorax section.

19. Round off the corners of the wing case with scissors.

20. Coat the wing case with five-minute epoxy. Note the husky, robust profile of the finished fly, which imitates the crawling *Ephemerella* nymphs like the Sulphurs.

PALE SULPHUR HALF-AND-HALF CDC EMERGER

Hook: #14-18 Daiichi 1130
Thread: Light cahill 8/0 Uni-Thread
Shuck: Three lemon wood-duck fibers and brown Z-Lon
Abdomen: Dark brown mottled turkey-tail fibers
Rib: Fine gold wire
Thorax: Sulphur yellow Superfine dubbing
Wings: Dyed light dun CDC
Hackle (optional): Cream hackle dyed pastel orange or light ginger tied parachute style

SULPHUR HALF-AND-HALF CDC EMERGER

Hook: #14-18 Daiichi 1130
Thread: Light cahill 8/0 Uni-Thread
Shuck: Three lemon wood-duck fibers and brown Z-Lon
Abdomen: Dark brown mottled turkey-tail fibers
Rib: Fine gold wire
Thorax: Sulphur orange Superfine dubbing
Wings: Dyed light dun CDC
Hackle (optional): Cream hackle dyed pastel orange or light ginger tied parachute style

SULPHUR ALMOST DUN EMERGER

Hook: #14-18 Daiichi 1130
Thread: Light cahill 8/0 Uni-Thread
Shuck: Three lemon wood-duck fibers and brown Z-Lon
Abdomen: Sulphur Harrop Dry Fly Dubbing
Wing: Light dun Medallion Sheeting
Hackle: Sulphur CDC fibers
Thorax: Same as abdomen

PALE SULPHUR ALMOST DUN EMERGER

Hook:	#14–18 Daiichi 1130
Thread:	Light cahill 8/0 Uni-Thread
Shuck:	Three lemon wood-duck fibers and brown Z-Lon
Abdomen:	Pale yellow Harrop Dry Fly Dubbing
Wing:	Light dun Medallion Sheeting
Hackle:	Pale yellow CDC fibers
Thorax:	Same as abdomen

PALE SULPHUR THORAX DUN

Hook:	#14–18 Daiichi 1100
Thread:	Light cahill 8/0 Uni-Thread
Tails:	Yellow Microfibetts
Abdomen:	Yellow turkey biot
Thorax:	Sulphur yellow Superfine dubbing
Wings:	Dyed light dun CDC
Hackle:	Honey dun or pale ginger

ORANGE SULPHUR THORAX DUN

Hook:	#14–18 Daiichi 1100
Thread:	Light cahill 8/0 Uni-Thread
Tails:	Yellow Microfibetts
Abdomen:	Sulphur orange turkey biot
Thorax:	Sulphur orange Superfine dubbing
Wings:	Dyed light dun CDC
Hackle:	Cream dyed light pastel orange or honey dun

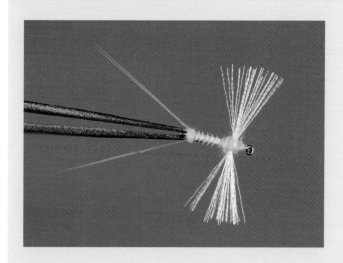

PALE SULPHUR DNA SPINNER

Hook: #14-18 Daiichi 1100
Thread: Light cahill 8/0 Uni-Thread
Tails: Cream Microfibetts
Abdomen: Light cahill turkey biot
Thorax: Sulphur orange Superfine dubbing
Wings: Shrimp DNA Frosty Fish Fiber

SULPHUR DNA SPINNER

Hook: #14-18 Daiichi 1100
Thread: Light cahill 8/0 Uni-Thread
Tails: Yellow Microfibetts
Abdomen: Yellowish tan goose biot
Thorax: Amber Superfine dubbing
Wings: Shrimp DNA Frosty Fish Fiber

Note: To imitate female spinners with egg sacs, use a ball of Sulphur yellow Superfine dubbing to separate the tailing fibers and keep them in place. This should be thicker than the abdomen.

6

Large Drakes and Extended-Body Dry Flies

Their graceful anatomy, however, has made them the primary target for fly-tyers with enough ambition and desire to create artificials that in appearance are extremely realistic-looking.

POUL JORGENSEN, *MODERN FLY DRESSINGS FOR THE PRACTICAL ANGLER*

One fly-tying challenge over the years has been to design an extended-body dry fly to imitate the larger species of mayflies such as Green and Brown Drakes (*Ephemera*) and the *Hexagenia*. Over the centuries tiers have developed a number of approaches to tying them. The extended body, which incorporates a shorter shank hook and lightens the overall weight of the fly, also imparts a more realistic-looking curvature of the fly's body—but extended-body flies also present several problems, both at the vise and on the stream.

Extended bodies have typically been crafted on a core that is attached to a shorter shank hook on which the rest of the pattern is tied. The core material for an extended body permits the tails to be fastened to it and some type of a body material to be wrapped around it to give the extension support and shape. If you leave a short

Hatches of the large drakes such as the Green and Brown Drakes are famous for bringing even the larger fish to the surface to feed on them. BARRY AND CATHY BECK

A male Ephemera guttulata *spinner, commonly known as the Coffin Fly.*

A female Green Drake dun rests on streamside foliage along Pennsylvania's Penns Creek.

section of core material bare, you can easily fasten the extension to the hook shank.

The core of the fly often becomes the core of the problem. Cores have taken many forms over the years: sections of silkworm gut, feather quills, wire, and even porcupine quills. When the core of the fly's body is made from a rigid material, it becomes much simpler to dress because a solid base does not move or bend. On the stream, however, the stiff body extension prohibits hooking the fish unless the fly is positioned correctly in the fish's mouth.

Designing extended bodies on softer cores is difficult. One of the most ingenious approaches that I've ever seen was developed by Ernest Schwiebert. Schwiebert stretched several feet of piano wire between two vises mounted onto his tying bench so that they were facing one another. On the taut wire, he tied a series of fly bodies down the length of the wire, leaving a gap between each fly. He then clipped each body free from the others by trimming the wire closely under the tail fibers and

leaving a short length of bare wire at the end of the body to allow it to be lashed to a hook shank. The bodies lacked the stiffness of more rigid core materials and hooked fish well. Schwiebert was an incredible fisherman and fly tier, and his Schwiebert Drake remains an ingenious method to create an extended-body fly.

Two renowned fly tiers who developed a technique for extended bodies using whole feathers were Harry Darbee of Roscoe, New York, and Chauncy Lively, from Pennsylvania. Darbee originated the Two-Feather Mayfly, which used small duck-flank feathers to create extended bodies. To create the extension, he clipped the central quill of a duck-flank feather near the tip to form a V notch. Pulling all of the remaining fibers except two toward the base of the feather, he bonded them in that reversed position by tying the feather to a short-shank hook. The remaining tips of the flank feather, pulled into an upright position, resembled a typical Catskill-style dry fly. Winding a good dry-fly hackle in the conventional manner completed the pattern. The body extension, due

A less common mayfly: Litobrancha recurvata, *or the Dark Green Drake. Large-size mayfly duns and spinners offer the creative tier plenty of room to experiment with the imitation of extended-body dry flies.*

to the naturally curved duck-flank feathers, curved like a mayfly dun. The two flank fibers left in their original position imitated the tails of the fly nicely.

Chauncy Lively used Darbee's technique with stiff rooster hackles instead of duck flank feathers but omitted the remaining feather tips that represented the wings. Once the feather fibers were combed back along the hackle stem, he coated them with a light film of flexible cement to preserve the shape of the extension. The flat-bodied profile of the Lively patterns was better suited to imitating spent mayfly spinners than the curved Darbee patterns. The 1980 book, *Chauncy Lively's Fly Box*, features several innovative patterns he designed using this method to imitate the *Isonychia* spinners and the Coffin Fly. Although the approaches of both men resulted in light flies that hooked more fish than fly patterns using a more rigid form of core, neither technique enjoyed much popularity.

Doug Swisher and Carl Richards present another concept in *Selective Trout*, published in 1971. Their pattern has an extension made by lashing hollow deer hair along the length of the fly's thorax and abdomen with criss-crossed turns of tying thread. Mike Lawson of Idaho further refined and later popularized the technique by tying elk hair, which is more durable than deer hair, forward beyond the eye of the hook and then folding the hair backward and binding it together with tying thread over a core of nylon monofilament.

After years of experimentation I settled on Joe Endy's technique of creating extensions made from foam on thin sewing needles, which are then removed when the extended body is complete. These extensions are easy to make, float like a battleship, and are durable. Lifelike and lacking the stiffness inherent in most extensions, they hook fish as easily as conventionally tied flies. I've used this technique to make everything from damselflies to grasshopper patterns. The foam required for this design is available at fly and craft shops in an array of colors that are perfect for many fly imitations. To make them more realistic you can add detail and color with permanent markers.

TYING THE GREEN DRAKE EXTENDED DUN

GREEN DRAKE EXTENDED DUN
(*Ephemera guttulata*)

Hook:	#10-12 Tiemco 2488 or 206BL
Thread:	White 8/0 Uni-Thread
Tails:	Three black moose hairs
Body:	White foam strip
Thorax:	White Superfine dubbing
Wings:	Olive CDC and light olive dyed teal flank or guinea mixed
Hackle:	Grizzly dyed pale olive and tied parachute style

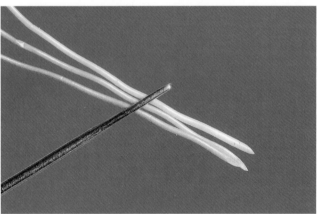

1. Select three long, straight moose body hairs. Hold the hairs close to their butts and trim the ends at a hard angle. Moose body hair is hollow, which will compress under thread pressure, yet allows expansion when the body is removed from the arbor. The hair is the right diameter for tailing larger flies and is reasonably tough. Thread the hairs through the eye of a fine diameter sewing needle.

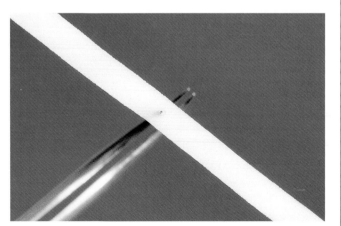

2. Cut a strip of white closed cell foam approximately ⅛-inch wide by 2½ inches long with a paper cutter or craft shears.

3. Push the needle through the foam strip in the center.

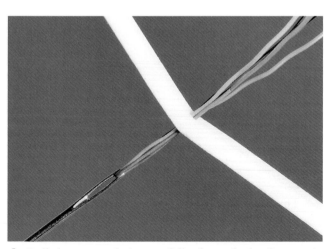

4. Pull the moose hairs carefully through the foam strip with the sewing needle.

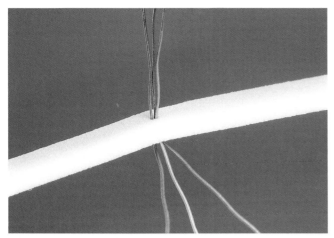

5. Remove the sewing needle carefully.

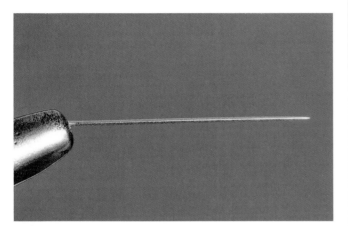

6. Clamp the sewing needle in the vise by the eye.

7. Thread the foam/moose hair assembly onto the needle so that the tips of the moose hair are pointing back over the vise jaws. Even out the tips of the hairs and adjust the length. The tail fibers should be approximately 1 inch long.

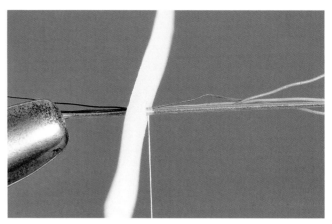

8. Attach light cahill 8/0 thread to the needle to the right side of the foam. The thread should go around both the moose hairs and the needle. Do not trim the moose hairs.

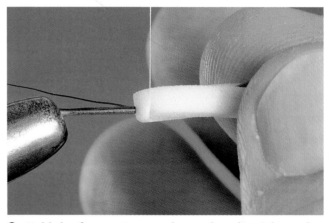

9. Fold the foam strips together and to the right so that they surround the needle and the butts of the moose hairs. The tying thread will be hanging down between the foam strips. Bring the thread up on the side closest to you, approximately 3/32-inch from the folded end of the foam strip.

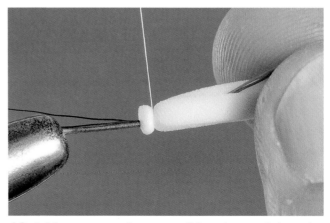

10. Make one complete turn of thread around the strips at this point and pull tight. Take a second turn so that the thread is again hanging below the needle.

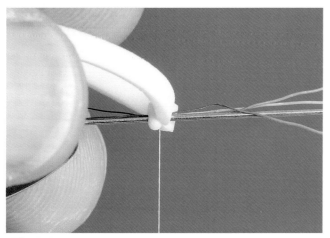

11. Pull the free ends of the foam strip back to expose the sewing needle and moose hairs.

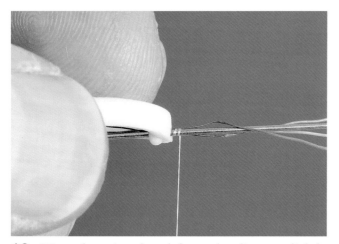

12. Wrap the tying thread forward a distance slightly greater than the first body segment.

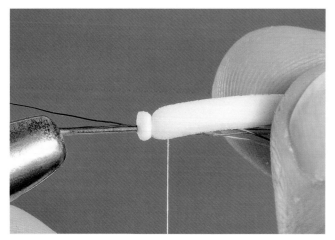

13. Fold the foam strip ends forward again along the sewing needle.

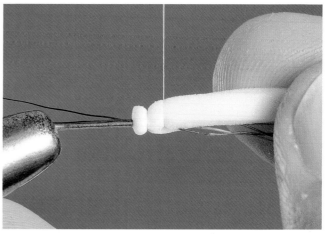

14. Wrap the tying thread around the foam and pull tight to form the second segment.

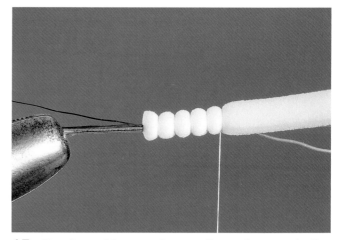

15. Continue this procedure until you have made five body segments.

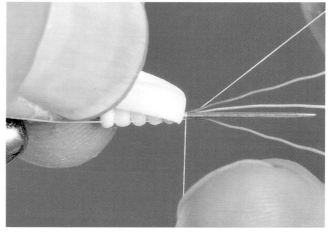

16. Spread the foam strip ends and whip-finish over the hairs and needle. Trim the thread off, but do not cut the hair butts yet.

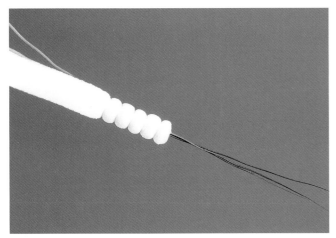

17. Carefully twist and slide the foam body extension off the needle and put it aside.

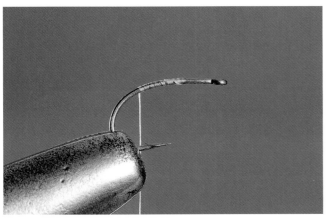

18. Clamp a 2XS wide-gap hook in the vise and attach light cahill 8/0 thread at the midpoint. Wrap the thread to a point over the end of the barb.

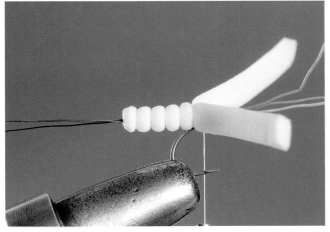

19. Spread the foam strip ends of the extension and bind the moose hair butts securely to the hook shank.

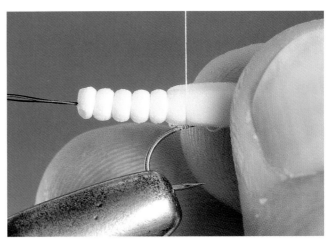

20. Bring the foam strip ends together again and build two more segments on the hook shank as you did on the needle.

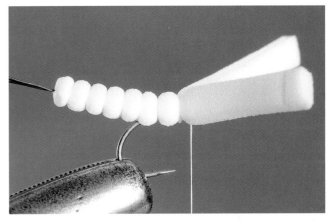

21. You can impart a nicely tapered transition to the body by spacing the distance between segments and by stretching the foam strips forward before taking a turn of tying thread

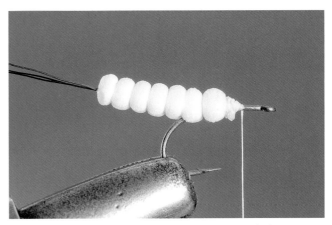

22. Trim the butts of the foam strips and the moose hairs.

23. Select two large CDC feathers dyed olive and even out the tips. Bind the stacked feathers down with the tips pointing forward over the hook eye. The wing should be the same length as the body.

24. Trim the butts of the CDC feathers closely.

25. Pull the wing upright and then take a few turns of thread in front of it followed by a few around the base. For a wing veil select a large guinea or teal feather dyed pale olive and cut a V notch in the tip.

26. Introduce the notched feather from under the fly so that half of the fibers are on each side of the wing post and fold them so that they are flat against the sides of the wing.

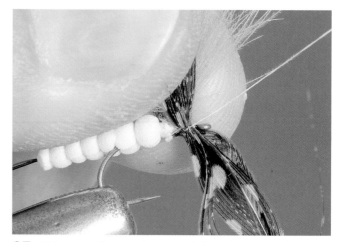

27. Take two diagonal turns of thread around the wing veil and the hook shank.

28. Take several firm turns around the base of the wing post and trim the butts of the wing veil.

29. Apply white Superfine dubbing to the thread and build the thorax behind the wing post.

32. Dub the head of the fly with white Superfine dubbing.

30. Select a grizzly hackle dyed pale olive and prepare it by stripping the webby fibers from the base. Tie in the hackle by the stem so that the bright side is facing up. Be sure to leave a short length of bare stem exposed.

33. Whip-finish and cut off the thread. Note that the posture and curvature of the abdomen is similar to a natural mayfly. The parachute hackle keeps the thorax of the fly close to the surface.

31. Take one open turn up the base of the wing post and wrap the hackle back down to the top of the thorax in close turns. Tie off the hackle on the hook shank in front of the wing and trim off the excess.

COFFIN FLY EXTENDED SPINNER
(*Ephemera guttulata*)

Hook:	#10-12 Tiemco 2488 or 206BL
Thread:	White 8/0 Uni-Thread
Tails:	Three black moose hairs
Body:	White foam strip
Thorax:	White Superfine dubbing
Wings:	Black DNA Frosty Fish Fibers
Hackle:	Dark pardo Coq de Leon or dark grizzly tied parachute style

BROWN DRAKE EXTENDED DUN
(*Ephemera simulans*)

Hook:	#10-12 Tiemco 2488 or 206BL
Thread:	Tan 8/0 Uni-Thread
Tails:	Three black moose hairs
Body:	Dark tan foam
Thorax:	Dark tan Superfine dubbing
Wings:	Natural brown CDC and dark brown partridge fibers
Hackle:	Cree or ginger and grizzly mixed and tied parachute style

BROWN DRAKE EXTENDED
SPINNER (*Ephemera simulans*)

Hook:	#10-12 Tiemco 2488 or 206BL
Thread:	Tan 8/0 Uni-Thread
Tails:	Three black moose hairs
Body:	Light tan foam strip
Thorax:	Tan Superfine dubbing
Wings:	Smoke DNA Frosty Fish Fibers
Hackle:	Cree or ginger and grizzly mixed and tied parachute style

7

The Tricorythodes Hatch

The hatches must be seen to be believed. They last only an hour or two, but the number of insects present is immense, and the trout love them.

ED KOCH, *FISHING THE MIDGE*

*L*ong after the initial rush of the spring fishing season has subsided and the "glamorous" Green Drakes, Cahills, March Browns, and Hendricksons are but a memory, the longest mayfly hatch of the year is only just beginning. For anglers who are willing to be on the water at daybreak through the summer, the early morning hatches of *Tricorythodes* provide some of the most exciting and challenging fishing of the season. Though *Tricorythodes* are the smallest mayflies that most fishermen see on the stream with the exception of *Pseudocloeon*, they more than make up for their tiny size by hatching in astonishing numbers over a period of several months. To ignore them is to miss out on one of fly fishing's finest moments. On my home waters of southeastern Pennsylvania, superb Trico fishing often begins as early as mid to late June and, depending upon seasonal temperatures, can persist well into October.

The diminutive flies of the *Tricorythodes* genus—"Tricos"—are unique among all mayflies: the nymphs hatch into duns, molt into spinners, and return to the

Wes Osborne rigging for a morning's Trico fishing on Tulpehocken Creek near Reading, Pennsylvania. Long leaders, fine tippets, and well-placed drifts are critical to success in this type of fishing.

Daybreak on Spring Creek near Bellefonte, Pennsylvania. Tricorythodes *spinners will begin to fall on the water once the dew dries from their wings, attracting pods of feeding trout and providing exciting fishing for several hours each morning through the summer and into the fall.* BARRY AND CATHY BECK

water to lay eggs and complete the life cycle all within a span of several hours. In the east the male duns begin each day's hatch in the dark, predawn hours with the female duns hatching a few hours later, usually right after daybreak. Later in the season as the water temperatures begin to cool, the hatches will take place later in the morning. As do most other mayflies, the freshly hatched duns will fly off to streamside vegetation to mature and molt into spinners. However Tricos also often fly off to join the mating swarms of spinners in the air before this transformation is complete, and at times if you look closely at the water surface you will see the thin skins shed from the duns on the water as well as flies on the wing with the husks still partially attached to them. Clouds of adult flies can often be seen as high as 30 feet in the air. Mating swarms of thousands of flies glitter against the dark foliage as their wings reflect brightly in the low morning sun. The clouds of mating spinners will gradually begin to drop closer to the river's surface. By eight to ten in the morning, the male spin-

ners begin to fall spent onto the water, and not long afterward the female spinners begin to fall and deposit their eggs in the water.

The blackish male duns have high, oversize wings with a whitish tint, while the abdomen of the female duns is olive-gray and their thorax nearly black. As spinners, the males retain the dark blackish color, but the abdomens of the females become a chalky grayish white color with a black thorax. The overall profile of the body appears to be short and robust, and the thorax is thicker than those of most other mayfly species. Tricos have only a single pair of wings, while most other mayflies have a smaller secondary set of wings as well. The wings of the Trico are also much longer and wider than those of other species. The tails, light gray and long, are often three times longer than the fly's body. Matching the 3 to 4 mm length of these tiny flies is a critical part of fishing success. Al Caucci and Bob Nastasi, in *Hatches* (1975), observe that an error in matching the natural flies with hooks sized incorrectly by even one size in these small

A male Trico spinner is easily recognized by its dark-colored abdomen. Females have grayish white abdomens. Note the length of the tails in the spinners. While it is tempting to include long tails in an imitation, they can impede the fly's ability to hook fish as well as your ability to achieve a good drag-free drift.

sizes can result in a mistake of 30 percent in the length of the fly. To match the size of the flies accurately use #24 and 26 hooks.

Flies of the genus *Tricorythodes* and their cousins of the genus *Caenis* have frustrated fishermen for years with their tiny size and the difficulty of fishing their imitations, causing leading English writers to refer to *Caenis* species as the "White Curse." The early days of the Trico hatch bring moderate interest from the fish, and it isn't any more demanding than any other mayfly hatch. As the hatch progresses, however, the flies literally cover the surface of the water in the primary drift lanes. The fish respond to this smorgasbord with a feeding behavior that we do not see from the trout during any of the other mayfly or caddis hatches. At daybreak the trout will begin to rise higher in the water as they anticipate the morning's hatch and subsequent spinnerfalls. As the level of fly activity rises, the trout position themselves in choice drift lanes, hovering right under the surface. The trout will usually not move from this location much once they

have chosen a feeding position, and the larger fish will often become territorial of prime locations, chasing smaller fish away if they venture too close. As the feeding becomes increasingly aggressive the trout pod up in groups of three or four to several dozen fish that simply tip up and porpoise flies. The sight of dozens and dozens of fish positioned in plain view right under the surface taking flies in such a greedy manner is one of fly fishing's incredible experiences. At times when everything is quiet you can often hear pods of fish feeding. The spinners fall until about 10:30 in the morning, and the average trout will ingest hundreds of these flies in a single morning's feeding. Trout will often have a number of flies covering the insides of their mouths, throats, and gills.

Surprisingly, fishing during the height of the *Tricorythodes* hatches is some of the most difficult and demanding of the entire season. Trout in the course of an average morning see thousands of natural flies drifting by and form distinct visual images or patterns that they expect to see on the surface film. As the hatch continues over a

Tricos, found on freestone and limestone spring creeks, provide great fishing for several months each summer and early fall.
GAVIN ROBINSON

period of months, the fish become increasingly selective due to the steady daily parade of thousands of drifting naturals on the stream surface combined with the level of fishing pressure, and in spite of their almost greedy feeding behaviors, trout show an uncanny ability to detect and reject our flies.

To be effective against the ultraselectivity that often occurs during this spectacular hatch, I've experimented with a wide array of materials and tying techniques. While the bodies and tails of these flies are fairly simple to imitate, the wings are the most difficult, and likewise the most important, part of the artificial. For Marinaro, the dun's upright wings become the critical focal point or trigger for the trout as this feature is the first to appear in the fish's window of vision. Likewise, when the trout begin to shift their feeding preferences toward spent and dying spinners, the bright light pattern created by the wings and their contact with the surface film become the most critical part of effective and successful imitation.

Over the years I have worked with a variety of materials for imitating the Trico's wings and have had a lot of

fun experimenting with them in the process. I've used just about everything imaginable to create the effect of the spinner's wings, including CDC, snowshoe rabbit fur, hackle, hackle tips, Krystal Flash, and even Saran Wrap and sandwich bag material. I now tie nearly all of my Trico patterns with white or light dun Z Lon yarn, which reflects highly and creates the illusion of width due to the crinkly texture and does not have the inherent stiffness of other materials and the subsequent problems with castability. Z-Lon also creates a light pattern on the surface that is similar to the natural's. CDC makes a nice post wing for a dun pattern that is useful when conditions make it hard to track your pattern's drift.

The surface of any stream is an interplay of complex currents that deflect, swirl, and change patterns as the water passes over and around various permanent objects in the stream. Add to this numerous trout hovering right under the surface in active feeding patterns and the additional distortion of those currents created by their feeding activity, and maintaining a drag-free drift becomes more complicated than it would be with fish that are feeding more casually. The midge-size flies are more susceptible to drag unless we make a few adjustments in our fly patterns and tackle to minimize the effects of that current and any subsequent drag.

One way to minimize the effects of microdrag is to reduce the size of the fly. While we wouldn't want to drop from a size 26 to a size 28 hook as we would no longer be matching the fly's size accurately, we can alter the fly and achieve a better drift with less drag. At one time I tried to match every feature of the naturals as best as I could, including the their tails which are three times longer than their bodies. But by eliminating the long tails, we can greatly reduce the footprint on the surface and a lot of the drag we experience as a result of it. I no longer tie any tails on my Tricorythodes imitations, both dun and spinners, and have dramatically improved my success with these flies. Interestingly, the pattern to imitate the "White Curse" recommended by Frederic Halford over 100 years ago has no tails also.

Long leaders with supple tippets also help reduce drag. I use a hand-tied leader of 14 feet tapered to a long 7 or 8X tippet. This setup allows me to introduce more slack in the forward portion of the leader to help mitigate microdrag and also seems to provide some additional stretch to minimize break offs with these fine tippets. I like a butt section tied from a stiff nylon such as Maxima Ultra Green, which turns over a longer leader and helps maintain accuracy, and a tip section constructed from a softer nylon that introduces slack such as Orvis Super Strong or Frog Hair. The tippet can be cut back and a length of 8X added if conditions demand a finer tippet. Additionally, all of my fly lines for trout fishing have a permanent butt section of Maxima or Amnesia nail knotted to the tip with a perfection loop tied in the end to attach the leader.

In my opinion, many of today's graphite rods are too stiff to protect the frail 7X and 8X tippets needed to fish these flies successfully. Every year I see many fishermen who break fish off when setting the hook. I've used a variety of different rods for Trico fishing and find that the better rods are what most fishermen would characterize as a softer or slow action rod. While I have a number of rods in my own collection that fit this description, my favorite is a 6-foot, 6-inch cane rod for a 3-weight line I built several years ago. The taper was developed by Wayne Cattanach and has delicate tips that offer great protection for fine tippets, and I seldom break off a fish. The rod also has adequate backbone in the middle and butt to apply enough pressure to turn a good sized fish, and it has landed a number of trout up to 17 and 18 inches with fine tippets and tiny flies. The rod is matched with a little Hardy Featherweight reel, which has the super-smooth drag system that is critical to this type of fishing. I always play the fish from the reel. I also have several Winston BIIX series rods in 3 and 4 weights, which have worked well for fishing the Trico hatches when a longer rod is more useful to manage the drift.

The last issue to consider on tiny fly imitations is the hook. Prior to 1978, hooks available for midges were woefully deficient, and fly fishermen owe a great deal of gratitude again to Vince Marinaro for developing the first real midge hook. Partridge of England manufactured at Marinaro's request a modification of their successful Captain Hamilton bend in a miniaturized scale with a shortened hook point, widened gap, and an offset bend. The new model, the K1A Marinaro Midge, opened the door to tiny, #26-28 imitations that hooked fish well, even with a slightly turned down eye. The next great midge hook to arrive was manufactured by Varivas from Japan and marketed under the model number 988. The 988 was made with a 2X fine black wire with a 2X wide gap and a straight eye that hooks fish well. Sadly, Varivas is no longer manufacturing these fabulous hooks that our local midge fishermen were fond of, and I bought every package I could find when I learned they would not be available anymore. Hopefully someone will revive the 988 style in the future. Tiemco's 2488 is also an excellent choice with a short shank and an oversized gap that hooks fish well.

Ramsay's 14-Foot Midge Leader (7X Tippet)

.020 inch – 10 inches	.009 inch – 8 inches
.017 inch – 10 inches	.008 inch (3X) – 8 inches
.015 inch – 10 inches	.007 inch (4X) – 12 inches
.013 inch – 10 inches	.006 inch (5X) – 12 inches
.012 inch – 10 inches	.005 inch (6X) – 14 inches
.010 inch – 8 inches	.004 inch (7X) – 32 to 36 inches

A nice brown taken on a Trico spinner. The density of flies that can fall on the water often attracts larger fish to the surface to feed on them.

On a typical summer morning the pods of fish that form in the primary drift lanes at or near the surface to feed on the spent spinners will rise steadily until nine or ten o'clock depending on the air temperature. As the numbers of spinners drop off so will the intense level of surface feeding. Here and there fish will continue to feed sporadically especially in the calmer currents and eddies where spinners collect, but most fish will cease to rise. Even though this shift has occurred, there is still fishing to be had for the angler who is willing to change his approach. During the peak of the spinnerfall, the majority of the fish will be tipping at the surface to sip spinners and a floating pattern is certainly more effective, but as the spinner activity tapers off, the surface feeding activity will also drop off. Fish will still continue to feed on drowned or sunken spinners below the surface and present a good opportunity to catch fish with a sunken

spinner pattern and good sport can be had by changing to a subsurface approach after most of the other fishermen have left the stream. Even during the heavy spinner feeding on the surface a lot of feeding also takes place below, especially with the larger fish, making a sunken imitation an important variation to tie and fish. A spinner pattern tied with materials to help it to sink can be deadly, and a great method is to use a tandem rig and drop a sunken spinner pattern off of a dry pattern like an Adult CDC Caddis pattern to serve as an indicator. Attach the sunken spinner as a dropper with a foot of tippet material tied to the bend of the indicator pattern's hook with an improved clinch knot. My pattern to imitate a sunken spinner uses a wire body and a Cyclops bead for weight and changes the dubbing used on the floating patterns to one that will absorb water to help the pattern sink.

TYING THE PARACHUTE TRICO DUN

PARACHUTE TRICO DUN (Male)

Hook: #24–26 Partridge K1A or Tiemco 2488
Thread: Black 14/0 Sheer
Body: Natural dark dun Canada goose biot
Wing: White Z-Lon tied as a post
Thorax: Black Superfine dubbing
Hackle: Natural dun

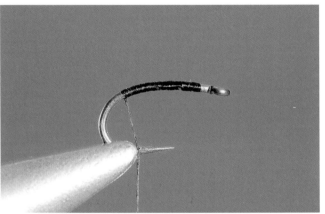

1. Clamp a wide-gap midge hook in the vise and attach 14/0 black thread at the midpoint. Wrap the thread toward the hook bend, stopping at a point just over the end of the barb.

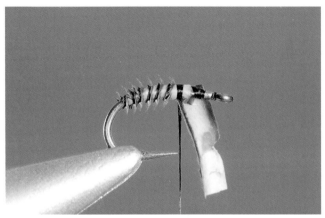

3. Wrap the biot away from you so that the raised edge of the biot produces a distinct segmentation. Wrap the biot just past the midpoint of the hook shank and tie it off. Trim the butt of the biot closely.

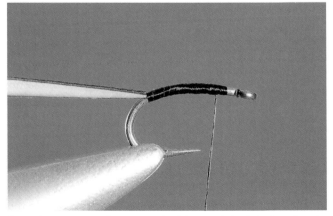

2. Select a natural gray goose biot and tie it in by the tip with the raised edge of the biot away from you.

4. Cut a section of white Z-Lon approximately one inch long and divide into two bundles with your dubbing needle. Place one of the bundles on top of the hook shank and tie down at its center with two firm turns of thread.

5. Raise the ends of the Z-Lon straight up and take two tight turns of thread around the hook shank in front of the post. Wrap up the post ¹⁄₁₆ inch and back down to the hook shank, stopping behind the post.

6. Apply black Superfine dubbing to the thread and build a thick thorax section behind the wing post.

7. Select a dark dun hackle and prepare it by stripping away the webby fibers at the base. Tie the hackle in so that the bright side is facing up and there is a section of clear stem exposed.

8. Wrap the hackle up the post in one turn and back down in close turns, one turn under the previous until you reach the top of the thorax.

9. Tie off the hackle tip on the hook shank in front of the post and trim off the surplus hackle. Dub a head in front of the post from black Superfine dubbing and then whip-finish and snip the thread.

10. Trim the post to a length equal to the hook shank. The Parachute Trico Dun is a good imitation of the dun stage but is also successful because many spinners drift considerable distances with the wings in a semi-spent position or with one wing up off the water surface. The bright and reflective Z-Lon post makes the fly easier to spot and follow through its drift.

TYING THE TRICO SUNKEN SPINNER

TRICO SUNKEN SPINNER

Hook:	#22-24 Daiichi 1130 or Tiemco 2488
Thread:	Black 14/0 Sheer
Head:	Black $\frac{1}{16}$-inch Cyclops bead
Tails:	Three light dun Microfibetts tied 2 to 3 times the body length
Abdomen:	Black Ultra Wire (small)
Wings:	Clear Medallion Sheeting
Thorax:	Blackish brown Harrop CEN Dubbing

At the end of the morning's spinnerfall when the trout begin to drop to deeper holding positions below the surface there is often continued feeding on spinners that have sunk due to currents, or become sodden. This spinner imitation, which is effective during the late stage of a spinnerfall, uses Medallion Sheeting to produce a well-defined wing profile; heavier materials like wire and a bead head help the pattern to sink.

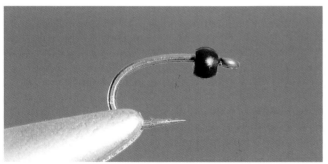

1. Thread a $\frac{1}{16}$-inch black Cyclops bead onto a 2XS, wide-gap hook and clamp it in the vise.

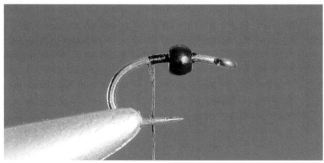

2. Attach black 14/0 thread behind the bead and wrap the tying thread toward the hook bend to a point just past the midpoint of the shank.

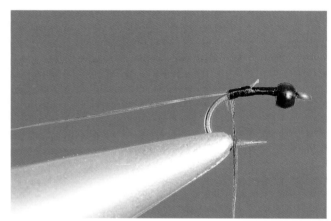

3. Select and tie in three light dun Microfibetts so that they extend two to three times the length of the hook shank. Wrap the thread toward the bend and stop at a point just over the end of the barb.

4. Wrap the thread forward to the bead and tie in a length of black Ultra Wire on the underside of the hook shank. Bind the wire tightly back to end of the thread base.

5. Wrap the Ultra Wire forward, each turn tight against the previous one, until you reach a point about the width of one bead behind the head.

6. Cut a strip of clear Medallion Sheeting one inch long from across the width of the material. From this cut a strip the width of the hook gap, cutting the material lengthwise. Twist the strip in its center to pinch it and create a tie-in point. Tie in the strip with figure-eight wraps of thread and fold the two ends of the strip back toward the bend.

7. Trim the wing to length by making a near vertical cut just past the fly's body and a second cut in a horizontal plane so that the finished wings equal the width of the hook gap. Round off the corners if you wish.

8. Apply a small amount of blackish brown Harrop CEN Dubbing and wrap a thick thorax behind and in front of the wings.

9. Whip-finish and trim the thread.

TRICO ALMOST DUN EMERGER

Hook:	#22–24 Daiichi 1130
Thread:	Black 14/0 Sheer
Shuck:	Black Z-Lon
Abdomen:	Black Superfine dubbing
Wing:	Clear Medallion Sheeting
Hackle:	Black CDC fibers tied as a collar
Thorax:	Same as abdomen

PARACHUTE TRICO DUN (Female)

Hook:	#24–26 Partridge K1A or Tiemco 2488
Thread:	Black 14/0 Sheer
Body:	Grayish olive goose biot
Wing:	Light gray Z-Lon tied as a post
Thorax:	Black Superfine dubbing
Hackle:	Natural dun

CDC TRICO COMPARADUN (Male)

Hook:	#24–26 Partridge K1A or Tiemco 2488
Thread:	Black 14/0 Sheer
Body:	Black Superfine dubbing
Wing:	Light dun CDC
Thorax:	Same as body

CDC TRICO COMPARADUN (Female)

Hook:	#24-26 Partridge K1A or Tiemco 2488
Thread:	Black 14/0 Sheer
Body:	Olive-gray Superfine dubbing
Wing:	Light dun CDC
Thorax:	Black Superfine dubbing

TRICO SPINNER (Male)

Hook:	#24-26 Partridge K1A or Tiemco 2488
Thread:	Black 14/0 Sheer
Body:	Black Superfine dubbing
Wings:	Light dun Z-Lon

TRICO SPINNER (Female)

Hook:	#24-26 Partridge K1A or Tiemco 2488
Thread:	Black 14/0 Sheer
Body:	Abdomen of natural black/white barred turkey biot fiber, thorax of black Superfine dubbing
Wings:	Light dun Z-Lon

8

March Brown Nymphs and Their Cousins

The nymph swims or crawls to shallow water and when ready to emerge, swims to the surface, wiggling to free itself of its case. This commotion attracts fish, and not being a fast swimmer, many are taken on their way up.

ART FLICK, *NEW STREAMSIDE GUIDE TO NATURALS AND THEIR IMITATIONS*

The trees were already turning green after a long winter, and the warm evening air was again beginning to fill with the dance of hatching mayflies above the riffles and pools of the little creek. Just upstream a ring left by a rising fish broke the pattern of the silvery currents as a light creamy tan-colored mayfly disappeared quietly in a swirl. In the next few minutes the fish took several more of these flies in regular succession; it took all of the composure a boy could assemble to knot the Gray Fox to the end of the leader.

The cast was an easy one, and the little fly landed quietly on the water just above the trout's last rise and was taken as soon as it drifted over the fish's holding position. The throbbing of the rod and the panic of the fish were over in a minute, and I held the brown for a moment, admiring its bright colors before allowing it to slide out of my hand, back into the cold water where it belonged.

Catching my first trout on a dry fly happened over 30 years ago, and the same scenario has played out many

A pair of March Brown nymphs in the water. Natural Maccaffertium, Stenacron, and Epeorus nymphs belong to the clinging nymph group, and their flat shape enables them to maintain their hold on the rocks in the fast currents they prefer.

Above: Nymph patterns tied to imitate March Brown and Light Cahill nymphs. The techniques used here create a realistic flat profile. JAY NICHOLS

When tying a batch of flies that require a secondary treatment such as epoxy back nymphs or Copper Johns, I place the flies on the edge of a foam block with their points buried in the foam. This holds them until I'm ready to apply and cure the epoxy before storage in my fly boxes. This also works well for flies that require several coats of varnish to achieve a nice glossy head. To save time I often tie a batch of these flies and coat them all at the same time. JAY NICHOLS

times since then. While every fish I catch still brings out the same boyish excitement for me, nothing can ever replace the feeling of satisfaction and the triumph of catching your first trout on a dry fly. Every time I drive past that pool, the image of that incident comes back vividly in my mind like it happened just yesterday. The hatching flies were what were known at the time as the Gray Fox, or *Stenonema fuscum*, which has since been reclassified as *Maccaffertium vicarium* and still ranks as one

of my favorite mayfly hatches to fish, along with its cousin species, the lighter cream-colored Cahills of *Maccaffertium ithaca* and the *Stenacron* species.

The flies of the *Stenacron*, *Maccaffertium*, and *Epeorus* families and their clinging nymphs provide some of the most anticipated and exciting fishing of the year for several reasons. After a long winter spent tying flies or building a new rod, reading by the fire, fussing with tackle, and adding new equipment to the collection, the first fish of

This wild brown fell for one of the author's March Brown nymphs. JAY NICHOLS

the new season is like a glass of cold lemonade on the hottest day of summer. Not only does it have a delicious and refreshing satisfaction for me, but the trout themselves seem to celebrate the change of seasons as well as the return of the mayfly hatches and rise to the flies with enthusiasm, having shaken off the chill of winter and its sluggishness like kids finally getting out to the playground again for recess.

Epeorus pleuralis is the first major mayfly hatch to appear on many of our eastern rivers in early to mid April and provides one of the first opportunities to fish to rising trout each year. This fly hatch served as the inspiration for the first truly American dry fly; the Gordon Quill, originated by the dean of American dry-fly fishing, Theodore Gordon, in the early 1900s. The spring season when the dark Quill Gordons begin to hatch is often unpredictable. I remember a crisp April afternoon years ago when the midday fishing saw a hatch of Quill Gordons, and here and there trout were beginning to rise to the emerging flies eagerly when all at once the snow began to fall heavily on Pine Creek in the middle of the hatch. And while it still feels like winter on some days, other days show the promise of warmer weather as

winter grudgingly gives way to spring. The trees are beginning to bud, skunk cabbage and watercress add a splash of long-awaited fresh green color to the wetland landscape, the robins and bluebirds have returned and are beginning to nest again, and the evenings in the east are treated to the chorus of the spring peepers.

Our other classic fly hatches of eastern mayflies belonging to this clinging nymph group are the beautifully speckled flies of *Stenacron* and *Maccaffertium*, which include *M. vicarium*, *M. ithaca*, *S. interpunctatum*, and a host of lesser species more commonly referred to by fishermen as the March Browns, Cahills, and Light Cahills. These species usually begin to hatch in May when the winterlike weather has completely passed, and the warmer days and cool evenings are some of the most pleasant and refreshing of the entire year. These flies will hatch from mid May through the middle of June and can always be counted on to provide exciting fishing, as the rises of fish are often aggressive as they try to capture the duns hopscotching across the surface trying to gain flight.

All the nymphs of these mayfly species are classified as clingers. These mayfly nymphs occupy the strongest flows of our rivers and streams and are well suited to that

A beautiful pool on the famous Slate Run in north central Pennsylvania is a good example of prime fast-water habitat for the nymphs in the clinger group. BARRY AND CATHY BECK

turbulent environment because of their flat, streamlined shape. The nymphs' wide, flat heads act like spoilers to deflect the strong currents over their bodies, legs, and featherlike gills and allow them to move freely without fighting the flow. The nymphs' bodies are also flat on the underside, which allows them to stay close to the rocks they live on. The legs are wide and flat, and the tails of the nymphs are much longer and thicker than those of any other mayflies and are held out in a widespread position like outriggers to assist the nymphs in maintaining their balance. These characteristics enable the flat nymphs to live in faster, more turbulent waters than the other mayflies and scuttle about freely on the stones while almost being pressed onto them by the strong currents. From an overhead view, the nymphs of *Stenacron, Maccaffertium,* and *Epeorus* appear almost triangular in shape, beginning with the widened head, and tapering sharply down to the bases of the tails.

When the nymphs are mature and ready to hatch they will migrate to shallower water where they become more readily available to the trout. *Epeorus* differs from most other mayfly species by hatching on the bottom of the streambed and swimming to the surface as hatched duns, making the nymph and its imitation relatively unimportant to the fisherman other than in the mornings prior to the beginning of the day's hatch. The angler fishing the early stages of an *Epeorus* hatch is more effective fishing a traditional wet fly like the classic Gold-Ribbed Hare's Ear or a soft-hackle. The *Stenacron* and *Maccaffertium* nymphs on the other hand swim to the surface and will drift for a considerable amount of time and subsequent distance before they shed their nymphal skins and take to the air. This trait makes them readily available to the fish, more so than many other mayfly species, and makes the nymph imitation an important component in your box. Often fishermen confuse or misinterpret the feeding activity of rising fish, believing that the trout are taking emerging duns, when in reality the fish are keying on drifting nymphs just under the surface or in the film. Trout keying on drifting nymphs and emergers will be looking upward at the flies as they drift over and will rely heavily on the silhouettes of the naturals to make decisions when feed-

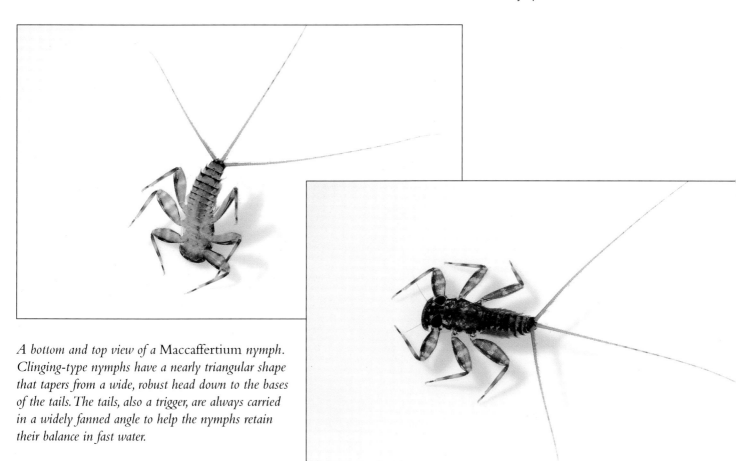

A bottom and top view of a Maccaffertium *nymph. Clinging-type nymphs have a nearly triangular shape that tapers from a wide, robust head down to the bases of the tails. The tails, also a trigger, are always carried in a widely fanned angle to help the nymphs retain their balance in fast water.*

ing. Our imitations need to focus on and impart the critical or trigger features of the natural to be successful.

One of the oldest patterns developed to specifically imitate these nymphs is the March Brown nymph that Art Flick describes in his *Streamside Guide*.

While the Flick March Brown has stood the test of time and is an easy fly to dress, it falls short of being a good imitation on selective fish for several important reasons. The clinger-type nymphs keep their tails widely spread at all times for balance. Capture a few and drop them into a container with water to see this behavior. The pheasant tail fibers used in the traditional pattern are weak and collapse in the water; too soft to remain in a widespread arrangement, they fail to reproduce an important part of the nymph's profile and a behavior that the trout key on. The fly's second major deficiency is the shape of the head, which is thin and much unlike the natural nymph's. Traditionally tied nymph patterns, like nearly all traditional dry flies, wets, and streamers, complete the dressing with a head tied in the standard method, built from thread. This thin tapered head doesn't simulate the wide, flat, pronounced head profile of the natural and ruins the overall silhouette of the finished fly. The best pattern to imitate these fly species, I believe,

came from Oliver Edwards of Yorkshire, England. In *Fly-tyers Masterclass* (1995), he showed tiers how to produce a wide, flattened head profile with his Heptagenid Nymph. Though this pattern is cleverly conceived and realistic in the hand, it is difficult and time-consuming to make. I watched Edwards dress one of these nymphs at a show years ago and was impressed with his thoughtful workmanship but realized I would never be able to offer this costly pattern to my customers. I needed to get the effect I wanted without making it too time intensive.

The solution came to me a few years ago when tying a batch of stonefly nymphs, which have the same wide head. I use a reverse method with Thin Skin for folded wing cases and lastly for the head of the fly. I tie in a strip of the material directly behind the eye of the hook and make a wide head by first applying the dubbing material as a base, pulling the film back over the top of the dubbing, and then tying it down into place. On the stonefly pattern I cut the Thin Skin close to the tie-off point, but I soon realized that it could be left intact and instead trimmed to shape to make the wing case as well. The effect was perfect for simulating the wing case and much more durable than traditional feathers. To better mimic the tails, I substituted moose hair, which is black but gets

*The Quill Gordon nymph (*Epeorus pleuralis*) is another important species within the clinging nymph group and is easily recognizable because it has only two tails, while all other members of the group have three.*

*A freshly hatched female March Brown dun (*Maccaffertium vicarium*).*

gradually lighter in color closer to the hide. Once bleached, the hair turns a shade of ginger that perfectly matches most of these flat-bodied nymphs and also is stiff enough to create the widely splayed effect without being so stiff as to cause the fish to reject it. Tough moose hair can withstand a fair amount of abuse. Dub the body and abdominal sections from dyed hare's ear or Harrop CEN Dubbing, which is blended for spikiness and ribbed with dark reddish brown wire to create segmentation and add some additional weight.

The Mayfly Clinger's pronounced flatness, tapered triangular profile, and widely spread tails effectively imitates the actual nymph's overall silhouette. Add a few to your fly boxes and dead-drift them upstream in the mornings at the time of the season when the flies are beginning to hatch. During the actual hatch, try resisting

the temptation to switch to a dry fly. Instead apply a floatant to this pattern and fish it in the film or as a dropper below a dry fly.

To dress these flies for fishing deep, lash a section of lead wire on each side of the bare hook shank to help achieve the pronounced flatness of the natural. For flies to fish in the film, you can substitute 20-pound-test leader material for the lead wire. Pick out the dubbing on the sides of the abdomen to simulate the gills. You can modify the Mayfly Clinger to match the *Rhithrogena* and *Epeorus* species nymphs by substituting a correctly colored dubbing. The nymphs of the *Epeorus* species are different from most other mayflies in having only two tails; while I don't think that the trout can count, it looks better to tie only two tails on the nymphs to imitate them.

THE EMERGENT MAYFLY CLINGER NYMPH

An imitation of a hatching March Brown nymph, one of the first mayfly emerger patterns ever written about, appears in the book *American Trout Fishing by Theodore Gordon and a Company of Anglers,* published in 1965 by the Theodore Gordon Fly Fishers. This book contains a chapter written by Ted Rogowski titled "Cracker Barrel Discourses." The cracker barrel group met regularly in the basement of Millie's Hairdresser Shop on 87th street in New York City. Several individuals who are now legends in the sport of fly fishing, including Harry Darbee, Charles DeFeo, Ernest Schwiebert, Keith Fulsher, Lee Wulff, and Vince Marinaro, attended. The cracker barrel regulars developed the Silk Stocking Nymph, a fly that features a wing bud constructed from a rectangular piece of a lady's stocking rolled into a cylinder and tied in at the front of the thorax. Another variation of this approach is to cover a small foam ball with the stocking material to gain a better float.

The clever concept simulates the folded wings beginning to unfurl as the nymph drifts along in the currents while emerging into a dun, and the tan-colored nylon stocking material creates the texture perfectly. "The most interesting way to fish this fly," Rogowski writes, "is to 'float' it half under and half upon the surface, breaking the tension of the water . . . the use of the emergent nymph for trout is no less a daring angling tactic, for when skillfully put to the trout, the rise of the fish at the surface is thrilling. And the emergent nymph is also the answer to those difficult fish which are not quite ready to take the dry fly, during that time betwixt and between, when the water begins to show floating duns but no trout will readily engulf your high riding imitations of them."

The emergent nymph is an important stage to imitate in the life cycle of the *Stenacron* and *Maccaffertium* species, and the mayfly clinger pattern is easily modified by tying in a wing bud before dressing the head of the fly and folding over the head covering/wing case material. While the stocking material for the original Rogowski emerger pattern might have been more entertaining to collect, an imitation of this important stage is one not to neglect in your fishing. My own imitations use a short wing bud of tan CDC feathers clumped and tied in together. The wing case material should be split up the middle or trimmed short to allow the CDC tuft to appear to be popping out of the nymph's wing case.

The author fishes a nymph on a small Pocono Mountains stream. You'll find mayfly nymphs of the clinger group in fast flowing riffles and pocketwater; drift imitations of them in likely runs and current seams. EMILY RAMSAY

TYING THE MARCH BROWN CLINGER NYMPH

MARCH BROWN CLINGER NYMPH
(*Maccaffertium vicarium*)

Hook: #12-14 Daiichi 1560
Thread: Camel 8/0 Uni-Thread
Tails: Three bleached moose hairs tied as long as the hook shank
Abdomen: Rusty Harrop CEN Dubbing
Ribbing: Wine metallic Ultra Wire (Brassie)
Thorax: Same as abdomen
Legs: Brown partridge hackle
Head: Same dubbing as abdomen
Wing Case: Mottled oak Thin Skin coated with five-minute epoxy

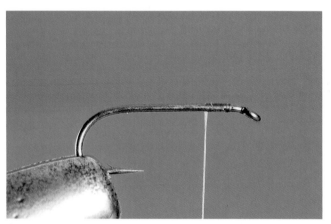

1. Clamp a 1XL nymph hook in the vise and attach 8/0 camel thread just behind the hook eye.

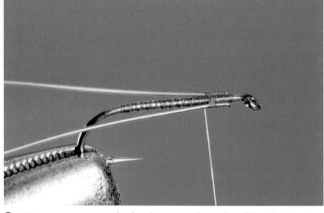

3. To create an underbody cut a length of leader material (.017-inch diameter for a #12 hook). Lead wire can be substituted for a pattern that you intend to fish deep.

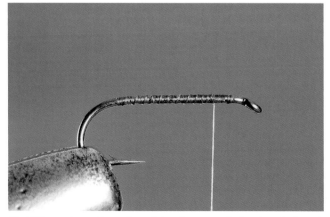

2. Wrap the tying thread back toward the hook bend, stopping at a point over the end of the barb and wrap forward in open spirals ¾ of the way to the hook eye to form a thread base.

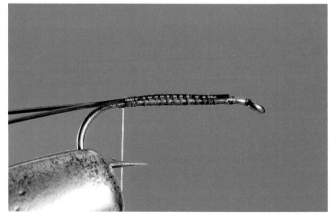

4. Lash the material to the sides of the hook shank, working your way back toward the bend. Continue to lash the underbody material back and stop just short of the end of the thread base.

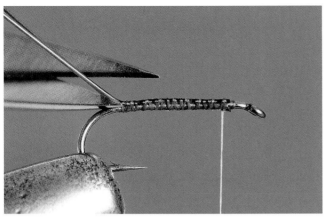

5. Trim the ends of the underbody even with the end of the hook barb.

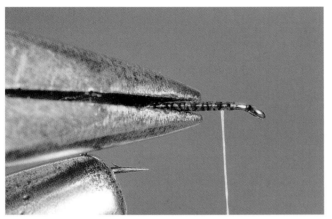

6. Using smooth-jawed needle-nose pliers or hemostats, press the underbody to straighten it.

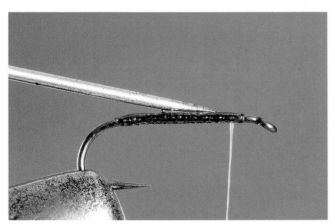

7. Coat the underbody with Zap-A-Gap and use the dubbing needle to distribute it on the top and bottom of the underbody.

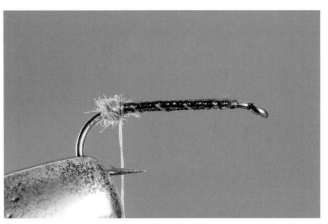

8. Apply a small amount of rusty Harrop CEN Dubbing and wrap a small ball at the end of the body.

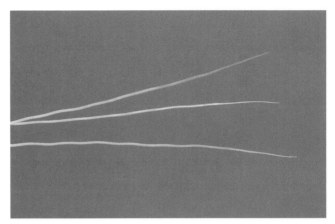

9. Select three straight bleached moose body hairs for the tails and even the tips.

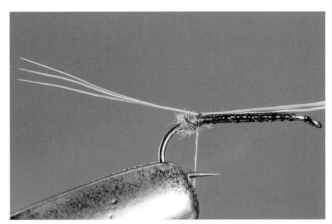

10. Tie in the moose hair tails so that they are the same length as the hook shank. Be sure the tail fibers stay on the top of the hook shank.

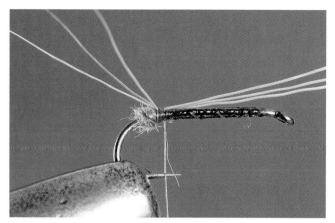

11. Wrap back toward the dubbing ball. Spread the outside tail fibers so that they angle at approximately 45 degrees to each other.

12. Bring the tying thread under the fly and up between the near side and center tail fibers in a diagonal wrap. The thread should continue over the top in front of the far side tail fiber.

13. Bring the thread under the hook shank and up over and between the center and far side tail fibers. Continue wrapping under the fly, passing over the hook in front of all three tail fibers. Place a small drop of cement at the bases of the tail fibers so they stay separated.

14. Wrap the thread toward the eye a short distance.

15. Tie in a length of wine metallic Ultra Wire and bind to the underside of the body wrapping back to the base of the tails.

16. Dub a tapered abdomen of rusty CEN Dubbing, stopping one third of a hook length from the eye.

17. Wrap the ribbing wire forward in even turns to the end of the abdomen. The wraps should be spaced approximately two wire widths apart.

18. Tie off the wire and break it off.

19. Use your dubbing needle to pick out the dubbing between the ribbing along the sides to imitate the gills for the length of the abdomen. Use the Velcro tool to brush out the gills along the sides.

20. The body should look like this when finished. The teased dubbing fibers simulate gills and enhance the flat appearance of the fly.

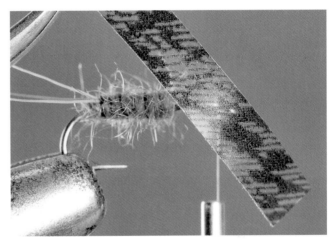

21. Cut a strip of Thin Skin approximately the width of the hook gap. Cut the strip across the width of the sheet.

22. Wrap the tying thread forward to the eye and orient the Thin Skin strip so that the shiny side is facing up and the strip is pointing out over the hook eye. Hold the strip tightly with the end against the hook eye and take one loose turn completely around it. Apply tension to pinch down the strip.

23. Trim the butt end of the Thin Skin strip and return the thread to the end of the abdomen.

24. Dub the thorax with rusty CEN Dubbing. The thorax should be twice the diameter of the abdomen. Leave an ⅛-inch area for the legs and head.

25. Select a small dark brown partridge hackle and cut a V notch in the feather to remove the tip. Stroke back the fibers on each side of the base of the feather so that 10 to 12 fibers remain on each side. Place the notched feather on top of the thorax, bright side up, and press in place with your left thumb. Tie the partridge in with several firm wraps of thread so that there is a section of the partridge feather quill on top of the thorax and the legs extend to the end of the hook shank. In this overhead view, note the section of feather quill extending beyond the tie-in point.

26. Dub the head with rusty CEN Dubbing, working from the eye back to the legs.

27. Pull the Thin Skin strip back over the head tightly and secure it with a few turns of thread.

28. Trim the wing case so that it is half the length of the abdomen/thorax area.

29. Flip the wing case forward and apply a drop of vinyl cement to the underside of it.

30. Use a dubbing needle to flip the wing case back over the legs and thorax.

31. Hold the wing case down with the butt of your dubbing needle to allow the cement to penetrate the leg fibers and thorax and lock the materials in place.

32. Spread the partridge fiber legs before the cement has a chance to set up while holding the wing case in position.

33. Coat the wing case with five-minute epoxy. The flat profile of the finished nymph and the wide head and wing case, along with the widely fanned tail fibers, make a well-defined target for trout.

LIGHT CAHILL CLINGER NYMPH
(*Maccaffertium ithaca, interpunctatum,* and other spp., *Stenacron* spp.)

Hook:	#14-16 Daiichi 1560
Thread:	Camel 8/0 Uni-Thread
Tails:	Three bleached moose hairs tied as long as the hook shank
Abdomen:	Golden brown Harrop CEN Dubbing
Ribbing:	Wine metallic Ultra Wire (Brassie)
Thorax:	Same as abdomen
Legs:	Brown partridge hackle
Head:	Same dubbing as abdomen
Wing Case:	Thin Skin coated with five-minute epoxy

MARCH BROWN EMERGING NYMPH

Hook:	#12-14 Daiichi 1560
Thread:	Camel 8/0 Uni-Thread
Tails:	Three bleached moose hairs tied as long as the hook shank
Abdomen:	Rusty Harrop CEN Dubbing
Ribbing:	Wine metallic Ultra Wire (Brassie)
Thorax:	Same as abdomen
Legs:	Brown partridge hackle
Head:	Same dubbing as abdomen
Wing Case:	Thin Skin
Wings:	Natural tan CDC feathers (paired)

Note: For this variation the wing case is split with scissors prior to folding back. The wing case should not be coated with epoxy.

9

The Slate Drake Nymph

It is another of the manifold enigmas of nature, and the fish are well aware of its existence, following the migrating nymphs into their primary hatching zones.

ERNEST SCHWIEBERT, *NYMPHS*

June evenings on the rivers and streams of the Appalachian Mountains are close to perfection. The days are pleasantly warm, and the threats of thunderstorms and showers are less frequent than in April and May. The nights are cool enough to make slipping into a sleeping bag soothing at the end of the evening after the conversation around the campfire has grown quiet, leaving only the soft background music of the river. Fly hatches, which have shifted to the evening hours in response to warmer water temperatures, increase not only

the number of hatching flies but also the number of species present, and multiple hatches often take place at the same time on the more fertile watersheds. During June evenings, caddisflies as well as an assortment of stoneflies often dance over the water on the purer streams.

The big green and brown *Ephemera* drakes make their dramatic appearances on many streams, and abundant numbers of Cahills still hatch over the riffles and pocketwater. The larger Blue-Winged Olives of *Attenella attenuata* and *Drunella lata* are often found hatching as well as

The Little Juniata River near Barree, Pennsylvania, is prime Isonychia *habitat.* Isonychia bicolor *has two emergence periods each year: one in June and a second in the fall.* BARRY AND CATHY BECK

Swift water like this section on Big Fishing Creek near Lamar, Pennsylvania, is another example of prime Isonychia *water. The nymphs are agile swimmers and success with imitations often requires adding movement to the fly to simulate this.*
BARRY AND CATHY BECK

the pale sulphur yellow and orange tinted flies of *Ephemerella dorothea dorothea*, which often bring a dramatic conclusion to the day's fishing on some of the calmer stretches. In the swifter runs, the fast-swimming nymphs of *Isonychia* genus dart nervously about toward the shallows where they clamber out of the currents and onto protruding streambed rocks and boulders to emerge into air-breathing mayfly duns. Stones that rise above the water line will often have numbers of stonefly nymph shucks on them as well as those from the fast swimming *Isonychia* nymphs. This emergence behavior marks the flies of the *Isonychia* species, also called the "Lead Wing Coachman," "White Gloved Howdy," "Dun Variant," "Mahogany Dun," and the "Slate Drake," as having one of the more unique emergence rituals among any of the mayfly species.

It was one of those warm and calm mid-June evenings years ago on a stretch of the Little Pine Creek. The Green Drakes were nearly finished for the year, and here and there freshly hatched Slate Drake Duns fluttered over the little river's surface. Several fish were already working along the edge of a current seam in midstream. I chose a dry-fly pattern from my boxes, which was developed on the Catskill rivers by Art Flick—a #12 Dun Variant—and knotted it to the end of the tippet with the anticipation that always fills one's thoughts when watching actively feeding trout. I touched the fly's hackles and tail fibers lightly with floatant and worked into position to try the nearest fish. The cast placed the Variant on the water lightly above the fish's position, and it drifted over the trout perfectly on the tips of its hackles without interruption. Several more casts met with the same resulting refusal, which came as a surprise as the drifts did not appear to drag and the fly looked good on the water, at least to my eyes. The other fish in the run shared the same lack of enthusiasm toward the dry-fly imitation as the first, with each fish refusing to rise to it. There's nothing in fly fishing that matches the high levels of frustration that are brought on by fish that ignore our best efforts, when we honestly feel that everything should be good

Brooding over Isos

The multiple emergences of *Isonychia* have been a source of debate and study over the years. Do they represent a true multi-brooded (bivoltine or trivoltine) life history or compose a single generation of flies emerging at different periods throughout the season (univoltine)? This "brood" behavior has been discussed in several important research papers. Some of this debate has its roots in earlier entomological texts written by J. R. Traver in the 1930s, which documented seven distinct species: *I. pacoleta, christina, circe, fattigi, harperi, matilda,* and *sadleri,* and another entomological study by Francis Walker, which identified *I. bicolor.* Other texts have identified a number of other species. Of these, *Isonychia bicolor, sadleri,* and *harperi* were generally given credit for being the most important species to both fishermen and the trout in most angling texts. The earlier season hatches of *Isonychia* were credited as comprising *bicolor* and *sadleri,* and the later summer and fall emergences were described as being represented by *I. harperi* in many of the older manuscripts. Later studies by entomologists Dr. Boris Kondratieff and J. R. Voshell (1984) concluded that all of the species identified by Traver are synonyms of the species *Isonychia bicolor* and should be treated as a singular species. A later paper written by David H. Funk and Bernard W. Sweeney of the Stroud Water Research Center, Academy of Natural Sciences, studied reproductive isolation between what they refer to as two distinctive forms of *Isonychia bicolor* found in White Clay Creek in southeastern Pennsylvania. Their research cites an earlier paper authored by Sweeney in 1979, which proved that *I. bicolor* is a truly bivoltine species, but their combined study makes a solid argument against the combination of previously recognized species due to differences within the life histories of specimens in their study. Their analysis determined that two distinctly different forms of *Isonychia* coexist in White Clay with differing coloration, shape of genitalia, and time of daily emergence. The form hatching in the early season was found to be bivoltine in behavior, with two separate generations hatching during the year, while another form hatched only in the later season and is univoltine with only one generation produced within the year.

enough (at least from our own perspectives) to achieve success. Standing in a pool of surface-feeding fish that seem uncatchable is a truly maddening experience.

The light was beginning to fade, and I needed to change tactics. In my box were several simple nymph imitations that were also developed years ago by Art Flick. These were tied with short peacock herl tails, a thin body of dark black-claret dubbing, and a collar of mottled brown grouse hackle to simulate legs. I quickly knotted the nymph imitation to the leader, cast across the current, and worked it with a hand twist retrieve. A few casts later there was a swirl near the surface and a strong pull as the brown literally hooked itself. The struggle was brief, and a minute later the fish wriggled free from my hand, darting for the safety of deep water. It was clear that the fish were not feeding on duns at all but instead were focusing on the nymphs swimming just under the surface.

While many nymphs spend the larval stage scuttling about on the stones and cobbles of the streambed and others occupy burrowed tunnels in the mud of the river's banks, the nymphs of the predatory *Isonychia* dart about from stone to stone in quick bursts much like that of a minnow. At rest, the sleek nymphs sit perched on rocks, maintaining their hold on the rocks with their middle and hind legs and holding their forelegs outward to help

The fast-swimming Isonychia *nymph is streamlined in appearance. Note the hairlike fibers on the leading edges of the forelegs. The nymphs will hold these legs outward at rest to help filter food from the current.*

gather food from the currents. The forward edges of the front legs are lined with long fibers along the forward margins to assist in collecting their food. When frightened, the nymphs move rapidly, moving their abdomens in an up-and-down motion for propulsion with their legs

A beautiful brown trout in spawning colors. Isonychia *enjoys a second emergence period in the fall when both the leaves and the trout take on their best colors.* GAVIN ROBINSON

tucked close to the thorax. At the time of emergence the nymphs seek out stones that protrude above the water line where they will climb out of the water onto dry land to hatch into duns. This behavioral trait slightly minimizes the importance of carrying dun imitations on the streams where there is an abundance of rocks for the nymphs to climb out of the water. On larger rivers where this is not as easy to achieve, the nymphs will hatch in more of a conventional manner at the surface.

The *Isonychia* species enjoy good distribution throughout the eastern and midwestern United States, and important populations live in many of our faster flowing streams. Emergences of these Slate Drakes occur in two peak periods each year; the first and the heaviest of these periods usually begins in mid June and continues into early July. A second emergence begins in late September when the water temperatures have returned to a more optimal level and can often run into mid October. Some streams have sporadic hatches of these insects throughout the midsummer months.

Before hatching, many nymphs begin to migrate toward the shallower sections of streams. Trout will begin to target these nymphs and a drifted imitation can be effective even when there is no visible hatching activity underway. When duns begin to show in the air, fishing a nymph pattern on the swing like a wet fly can be deadly. In calmer stretches, add action to the fly with either a hand twist retrieve, moving the rod tip through the swing, or by adding short strips of line as if you are fishing a streamer. Pay attention to the shallows and the edges of the stream as many fish will expect to find active nymphs in those areas. The *Isonychia* nymphs are large and average 14 to 15 mm during the earlier emergences, and they are matched well with a size 12 or 14 2XL hook. Later season hatches are noticeably smaller and average 10 to 12 mm in length. The three tails are short and feather-like. The nymphs' thin bodies are a dark reddish brown color, well segmented, and some have a distinct light-colored median stripe running the length of the dorsal surface. The legs are short and a richly speckled brown.

While creating an effective nymph imitation is not difficult, and you can certainly catch fish on simple fly patterns, the size and the unique profile and behavior of the naturals leaves room to experiment creatively to make a nymph that is more appealing and matches the natural nymph more precisely.

One of the more clever imitations I've seen was developed by tier Chauncy K. Lively and first appeared in the pages of *The Pennsylvania Angler* magazine where he wrote a fly-tying column for a number of years. His imitation had an abdomen made from a condor biot fiber, which does a superb job of duplicating both the segmentation and the gill structures that project at a near 90-degree angle from each body segment. Lively was a brilliantly innovative tier whose flies were a marvel of creative genius, and his techniques were both cleverly thought out and years ahead of their time. As a teenager I couldn't wait for the new issue of the *Angler* to see what his next article would feature. Sadly, Lively's patterns never gained the popularity they deserved, most likely because his flies were so complex and the techniques to tie them complicated, but fortunately for those that admired his work, the complete collection of his monthly articles were assembled into a book titled *Chauncy Lively's Fly Box: A Portfolio of Modern Trout Flies*, published in 1980. A well-worn copy sits on my bookshelf.

The *Isonychia* nymph pattern that I've settled on for my own use borrows from Lively's concept but uses a turkey biot dyed a deep reddish brown for the abdomen of the fly instead of condor quill biot, which is nearly impossible to locate unless you are fortunate enough to find a section of a wing quill at an estate sale of a fly tier. For the tails of the nymph, nothing seems to imitate the natural insect better than peacock herl. Fresh herls recently molted by the birds are rich iridescent bluish green in color, but when they are stored in the sunlight they will gradually turn more of a coppery bronze shade, which is a better match. To imitate the distinctive median stripe I use white Ultra Wire pulled over the abdomen and wing case. The wing cases on most of my nymph patterns are now made from Thin Skin coated with five minute epoxy to imitate the bulging wing cases of mature nymphs that have swollen because of the fully developed wings inside them. To create the movement of the natural as it swims I tie my imitations on the Daiichi 1770 Swimming Nymph hook, which does a great job of mimicking the swimming motion of the naturals when weighted on the forward half of the hook. The Tiemco 400T also serves well for this type of an imitation.

A second approach to imitating swimming nymphs like the *Isonychia* is to fashion an extended body from soft marabou fibers. By tying an abdomen from brown marabou fibers on a short-shank hook, you give the fly great movement in the water, and it is very simple to make. I prefer to use base marabou from feathers such as hen pheasant dyed dark brown, which is a finer fiber with more movement than larger marabou feathers. The marabou pulses and moves freely with every twitch imparted during its drift, and while not as accurately defined in terms of appearance, it makes up for this with its lifelike action in the water. The forward portion of the fly is dressed the same as the Swimming Isonychia pattern. The Isonychia Marabou nymph is a deadly combination of lifelike movement and realism.

The Swimming and Marabou Isonychia nymphs presented here are great patterns when fished deep as a search pattern or just under the surface during a hatch. When searching with the pattern, I often fish a pair of Isonychia nymphs on a 9-foot leader tapering to a 5X tippet. To the bend of the first nymph, I attach 18 inches of 5X with an improved clinch knot and attach a second nymph with a small split-shot centered between the two patterns. After making an up- and across-stream cast, I immediately mend upstream to allow the nymphs to sink deeper before beginning a hand twist retrieve.

TYING THE SWIMMING ISONYCHIA NYMPH

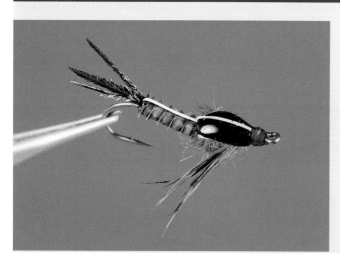

SWIMMING ISONYCHIA NYMPH

Hook: #12-14 Daiichi 1770
Thread: Wine 8/0 Uni-Thread
Tails: Three short tips of bronze-tinted peacock herl
Abdomen: Trico turkey biot fiber
Thorax: Dark claret brown dubbing
Wing Case: Black Thin Skin coated with five-minute epoxy
Median Stripe: White Ultra Wire (Brassie)
Legs: English grouse

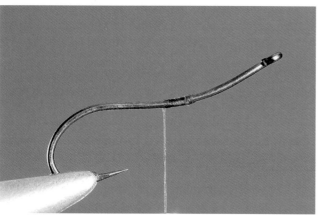

1. Clamp a curved swimming-nymph hook in the vise and attach wine 8/0 thread at the midpoint.

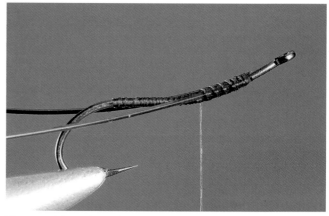

3. Double a length of .012-inch leader material and attach the ends to the sides of the hook shank.

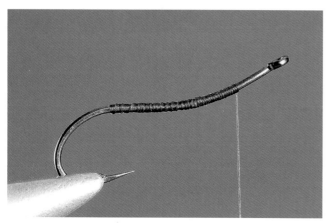

2. Wrap the tying thread toward the bend of the hook, stopping at a point over the end of the barb. Wind the thread forward three-fourths of the way to the hook eye to form a thread base.

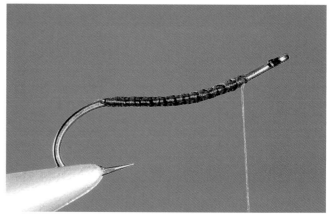

4. Wrap the nylon to the sides of the hook and back to the end of the thread base to form an underbody. Wrap forward over the underbody back to the forward ends of the nylon. Trim the excess material.

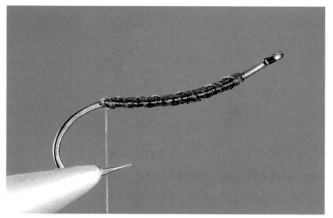

5. Wrap over the underbody again, working back to the tail end. Coat the underbody with Zap-A-Gap on the top and bottom sides.

6. Select three bronze-tinted peacock herls with nicely tapered tips and even them. Attach them to the top of the underbody so that they are approximately ³⁄₁₆-inch long. Trim off the excess herls.

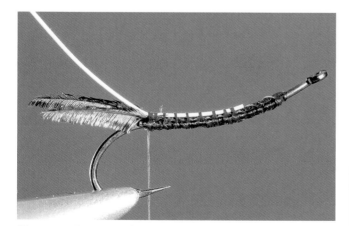

7. Wrap the tying thread forward just past the middle of the hook shank and attach a length of white Ultra Wire. Bind the wire to the top of the underbody, wrapping back to the base of the tails. Be careful to keep the wire centered down the middle of the underbody.

8. Select a dark reddish brown turkey biot and tie it in by its tip. The biot should be tied down flat with the raised-flue edge opposite yourself.

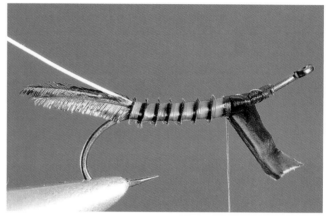

9. Grip the butt of the biot with your hackle pliers and raise it up so that it is perpendicular to the hook shank and the biot edge with the raised flue faces toward the tails of the fly. Wrap the biot forward in even turns, stopping at a point just past the midpoint, and tie off.

10. Pull the white wire forward and bind it tightly at the end of the abdomen to form a medial strip down the back of the body. Make sure the wire is centered on the top side of the abdomen.

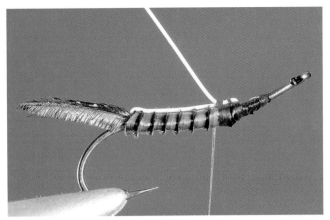

11. Fold the wire back over itself and bind it in place firmly.

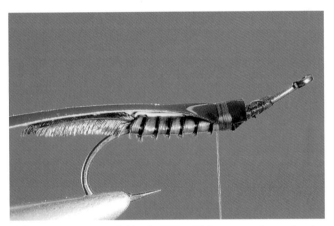

12. Cut a strip of black Thin Skin approximately the width of the hook gap and tie it in with the shiny side up and the strip pointing back over the body of the fly.

13. Build a thorax from dark claret brown dubbing. The thorax should be twice the diameter of the abdomen, and approximately ⅛ inch of open hook shank should remain.

14. Select a dark brown partridge or English grouse hackle and cut a V notch in the tip to remove the center quill. Stroke back the fibers at the base of the feather so that 10 to 12 fibers remain on each side of the feather.

15. Straddle the hook with the feather in front of the thorax and pinch the fibers against the sides of the thorax with your left thumb and forefinger. Take a complete turn of thread around the hackle fibers before applying tension. Take several more turns to anchor the legs firmly. Trim off the surplus hackle closely.

16. Pull the Thin Skin strip forward and tie it down to form the wing case.

17. Trim the excess wing case material.

18. Pull the wire forward over the wing case and tie it down securely. The wire should be centered on the wing case and aligned with the medial strip over the abdomen.

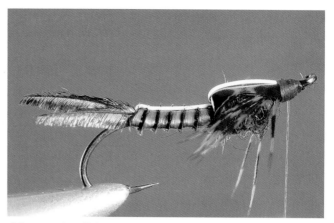

19. Break off the surplus wire.

20. Form a small head with tying thread and whip-finish. Trim off the tying thread and coat the head with cement.

21. Coat the wing case with five-minute epoxy. This nymph, streamlined like the fast-swimming naturals it imitates, emphasizes the defined medial stripe found on the dorsal surface of most of these nymphs.

TYING THE MARABOU ISONYCHIA NYMPH

MARABOU ISONYCHIA NYMPH

Hook: #12-14 Tiemco 2488
Thread: Wine 8/0 Uni-Thread
Abdomen: Dark brown marabou fibers
Thorax: Dark claret brown dubbing
Wing Case: Black Thin Skin coated with five-minute epoxy
Median Stripe: White Ultra Wire (Brassie)
Legs: Dark brown mottled partridge hackle or English grouse applied with the V-notch method

The Marabou Isonychia Nymph imitates the unique movement of fast-swimming nymphs in the water because marabou pulses and moves very well. The base marabou-like fibers for this type of fly are found on bird feathers such as the pheasants that have been dyed to match the naturals.

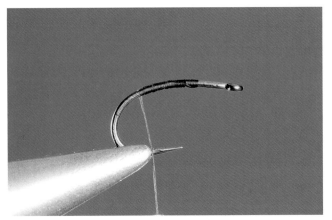

1. Clamp a 2XS wide-gap hook in the vise and attach wine 8/0 thread at the midpoint of the hook shank. Wrap the thread back toward the bend, stopping at a point just past the end of the barb.

2. Select a clump of dark brown marabou fibers and tie them in so that the tips extend back for a length equal to twice the length of the hook shank. Trim off the butts of the marabou fibers.

3. Cut a length of white Ultra Wire and tie it in on the top of the hook shank, wrapping back to the base of the marabou fibers.

8. Pull the wire forward over the center of the wing case to create a medial strip and tie it in place.

10. Coat the wing case with five-minute epoxy.

9. Break off the excess wire and form a neat head with tying thread. Whip-finish and trim off the tying thread. Coat the head of the fly with clear head cement.

Articulated Mayfly Nymphs

*Most fishermen become preoccupied with a twilight full of large fluttering drakes,
failing to grasp that fishing a nymph is better than a more obvious dry fly.*

Ernest Schwiebert, *Nymphs*

One of fly fishing's most celebrated events each year in the eastern United States is the emergence of the legendary hatch of *Ephemera guttulata*, the Eastern Green Drake, in late May or early June. Though these large insects bring many good trout to the surface, anglers willing to fish with nymph imitations during a hatch always have an opportunity to catch larger fish.

The nymphs of the *Ephemera, Ephoron,* and *Hexagenia* genus are burrowers who spend most of their lives in tunnels in the mud of the streams banks until just before emergence. The heads of these nymphs have a pair of small tusk-like appendages that help them to burrow, and their long, wormlike bodies have a sinuous movement while swimming to the surface to hatch. The forward half of their abdomens have thick, long, and feathery gills that

are constantly moving. The abdomens are usually mottled and slightly darker on the dorsal surface with well-defined segmentation, and the tails are relatively short and feather-like. The legs of the nymphs are relatively short and are held close to the thorax when the nymph is swimming.

The profile, physical characteristics, and behavior of these nymph varieties require a dramatically different approach from traditional methods to create an effective imitation. Mimicking the profile of these nymphs is simple as they are almost round in cross section and do not require an underbody to achieve that effect. However, imitating the motion of the natural is a challenge. In my opinion, nothing works better than using an articulated body approach with a hinged midpoint to replicate the naturals' swimming movement.

While hatches of big drakes can often bring larger trout to the surface to feed on emerging duns, many of the larger fish prefer to feed subsurface on the robust nymphs. BARRY AND CATHY BECK

Little Pine Creek in northern Pennsylvania has good hatches of Green Drakes. BARRY AND CATHY BECK

Articulated nymphs have been around for quite a while. The first ones I was exposed to were presented in Swisher and Richards' *Selective Trout* in 1970 where the style of a hinged body was referred to as a "wiggle" nymph. The theory behind articulating flies is relatively simple: an abdomen section dressed on the shank of a long hook (with the hook bend removed) is connected to a thorax on a separate hook by wire or strong thread, which permits the abdomen to swing in the water. However, the hinge system needs to be built properly for the pattern to be most effective. The best hooks to use are long straight shank hooks that have a round, straight eye. Eagle Claw and other bait hook manufacturers market light wire hooks for panfish with an Aberdeen style bend and a long shank that fills the bill nicely for making the abdomen sections of these nymphs. To make the fly move well, however, requires that the orientation of the eye in the completed abdomen section be in the same plane as the hook bend, not the hook eye, of the front hook. This will allow the most available movement of the nymph's abdomen in both directional planes—up and down as well as side to side. To accomplish this I select a hook that has slightly more shank length than needed to complete the abdomen section and clip off the bend of the hook before clamping it in the jaws of the vise.

Constructing and tying in the loop is critical. A loop that is not oriented correctly or is made from another material such as a soft wire will not allow your fly to move freely; improper mounting of this loop can hurt the performance of the hinge and make the fly lean to one side or the other. The name "wiggle nymph" is mis-

An immature Ephemera *nymph.* Ephemera *nymphs are burrowers, and the genus includes the celebrated* E. guttulata, *or Eastern Green Drake;* E. simulans, *commonly called the Brown Drake;* E. varia, *known as the Yellow Drake; the smaller flies of* Ephoron leukon, *known as the White Fly; and* Hexagenia limbata, *the giant Michigan Mayfly.*

leading. Despite a well-constructed nymph pattern with a hinged body, the fly will not wiggle as it is retrieved. Because of this I have chosen to call this style an articulated nymph instead.

The last important consideration is the heavy gills, as they are a definite trigger for a feeding fish. The materials used to make this type of nymph must be soft enough to create the illusion of fluid movement in the water. Philoplumes or after-shaft feathers are fragile but are also soft in texture and make a great representation of the pulsing gills lining the sides of the abdomen. When anchored in place with a feather strip overlay and ribbing wire, the end result is strong and creates lifelike movement when the pattern swims in the water. The natural tan-gray colored philoplume feathers found on the hen ring-necked pheasant look better than any other feather I have tried. Most philoplumes are of a bolder bluish gray tone that doesn't look quite as nice as hen pheasant does.

TYING THE ARTICULATED GREEN DRAKE NYMPH

ARTICULATED GREEN DRAKE NYMPH
(*Ephemera guttulata*)

Hook:	#10 Aberdeen hook trimmed to 11 mm (abdomen), #14 Tiemco 2488 (thorax)
Thread:	Yellow 8/0 Uni-Thread
Tails:	Three natural gray ostrich herl tips
Abdomen:	Olive yellow Harrop CEN Dubbing and natural mottled brown turkey quill
Rib:	Fine gold wire
Gills:	Natural gray philoplume
Thorax:	Same as abdomen
Wing Case:	Mottled oak Thin Skin and pearl Flashabou coated with five-minute epoxy
Legs:	Natural tan-brown hen pheasant hackle
Tusks:	Tannish yellow goose biot tips

1. Begin by cutting the bend from a #10 Eagle Claw 214 long-shank hook with diagonal cutters.

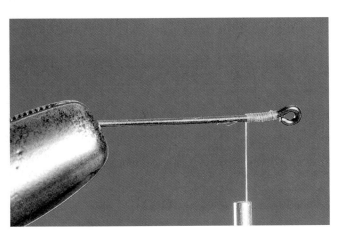

2. Clamp the hook shank in the vise at the end with the eye of the hook oriented in a vertical plane. Attach yellow 8/0 thread behind the hook eye.

3. Wrap the tying-thread back toward the vise jaws. Use a metric rule to determine the correct length of the extension (11 mm including the hook eye for a Green Drake nymph) and stop the thread at that point. For tails select the tips of three natural gray ostrich herls and even out the tips. Tie in the tails at the end of the thread base. They should be approximately one-half the length of the hook shank. Trim the excess herls closely.

4. Cut a strip of natural brown mottled turkey approximately ⅛ inch wide and trim off ½ inch from the tips. Tie in the turkey strip on top of the hook shank by the narrow end. The strip should extend back over the tails with the dull side facing up.

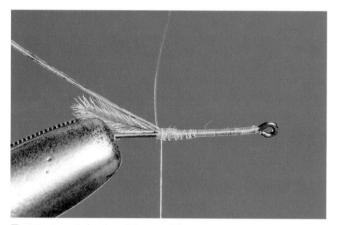

5. Tie in a length of fine gold wire.

6. Apply olive yellow CEN Dubbing to the thread and dub the first half of the abdomen. The abdomen should have a slight taper.

7. Select a gray philoplume feather from a hen pheasant and tie in on top of the hook shank by the midpoint. The butt of the feather should extend back toward the tail. Trim off the tip of the philoplume.

8. Dub the rest of the abdomen, leaving just enough room at the eye for a small head.

9. Pull the philoplume forward to the eye and tie off. It should sit flat on the top of the body.

10. Trim off the surplus feather.

11. Pull the turkey strip flat over the top of the abdomen and tie off at the eye. Trim off the surplus material.

12. Wrap the ribbing wire forward in even turns. Take care to wrap between the fibers of the philoplume.

13. Tie off the ribbing wire and break off the surplus.

14. Whip-finish a small head. Trim the thread and apply head cement. After the head has dried, carefully trim off the excess hook shank under the tails with wire cutters and set the abdomen aside.

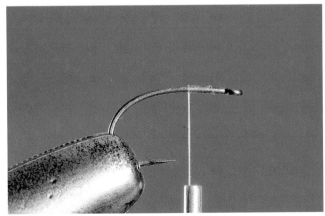

15. Clamp a short-shank, wide-gap hook in the vise and attach 8/0 yellow thread just behind the eye.

16. Cut a length of .010-inch or .012-inch stiff nylon leader material and thread it through the eye of the abdomen section.

17. Wrap the tying thread back toward the bend, stopping at a point over the end of the barb. Double the ends of the mono to form a loop and attach it to the front hook with a few turns of thread. Be sure that the legs of the loop sit flat on top of the hook shank. The trick is to orient the loop of nylon so that it is lashed to the hook in the same plane as the eye of the thorax on the front hook so that the abdomen section moves properly. As you lash the nylon loop to the front hook, adjust its final length by pulling the "legs" of the loop to shorten it, but not so much that it inhibits any movement of the rear section of the fly.

18. Bind the mono with firm turns of thread stopping just short of the hook eye. Trim the ends of the mono and coat with Zap-A-Gap.

19. Tie in a length of pearl Flashabou so that it is centered on top of the hook shank.

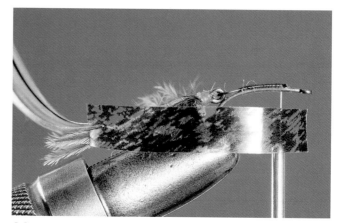

20. Cut a strip of Thin Skin sheeting approximately the same width as the hook gap.

21. Tie in the Thin Skin on top of the hook shank with the shiny side facing up. Hold the strip flat on top of the hook and take one loose turn of thread. Pull the thread tight to pinch it down and secure in place. Trim off the butt of the strip if necessary and take a few more turns of thread.

22. Select a marabou feather from a hen pheasant skin, or a feather with long-base marabou fibers. Cut a V in the center of the feather to remove the stem.

23. Stroke the fibers back together and use your thumbnail and your index finger to break the fibers so that they are even in length. Hold the prepared feather so that it sits flat on top of the hook shank with the fiber tips extending back far enough to cover the hinge. The notch should straddle the wing-case material.

24. Pinch the marabou fibers against the sides of the fly with your left thumb and forefinger and take one complete turn of thread around the feather. Pull the thread taut while holding the feather in position. Take several more tight turns to secure the fibers in place. Trim the butts of the feather and dub a full thorax of olive yellow CEN Dubbing, leaving approximately ³⁄₃₂" of open space at the eye.

25. Select a well-marked hen pheasant back feather, remove the tip, and stroke the base fibers back to leave 10 to 12 fibers remaining on each side of the stem. Straddle the thorax with the feather so that the fiber tips extend to the hook bend. Pinch the feather on the sides of the thorax with your left thumb and forefinger, take one loose turn of thread around it, and pull the thread taut. Take several more firm turns of thread and trim off the feather butt.

26. Fold the wing case, bring it forward over the thorax, and tie it down. Do not pull the material. The longer wing case appears more proportionate and hides the hinge. Trim off the excess material.

27. Pull the Flashabou strip over the center of the wing case and tie down. Trim off the excess.

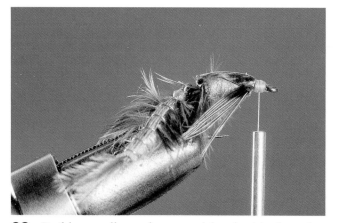

28. Build a small, neatly tapered head with the tying thread, stopping at the front of the wing case.

29. Select two fine tannish yellow goose biots and tie one on either side of the head to form the tusks and trim off the excess.

30. Coat the head with head cement and apply five-minute epoxy to the wing case. The gill technique coupled with the hinge method creates a nymph that swims with the fluid, pulsing movement characteristic of the burrowing types of mayfly nymphs.

ARTICULATED BROWN DRAKE NYMPH
(*Ephemera simulans*)

Hook: #10 Aberdeen hook trimmed to 13 mm (abdomen), #14 Tiemco 2488 (thorax)
Thread: Tan 8/0 Uni-Thread
Tails: Three natural gray ostrich herl tips
Abdomen: Golden brown Harrop CEN Dubbing and natural mottled brown turkey quill
Rib: Fine gold wire
Gills: Natural gray philoplume
Thorax: Same as abdomen
Wing Case: Mottled oak Thin Skin and pearl Flashabou coated with five-minute epoxy
Legs: Natural tan-brown hen pheasant hackle
Tusks: Tan goose biot tips

ARTICULATED WHITE FLY NYMPH
(*Ephoron leukon*)

Hook: #10 Aberdeen hook trimmed to 5mm (abdomen), #18 Tiemco 2488 (thorax)
Thread: Light cahill 8/0 Uni-Thread
Tails: Three natural gray ostrich herl tips
Abdomen: Cream Life Cycle dubbing and natural light mottled brown turkey quill
Rib: Fine gold wire
Gills: Feather-base marabou
Thorax: Same as abdomen
Wing Case: Mottled oak Thin Skin and pearl Flashabou coated with five-minute epoxy
Legs: Gray Hungarian partridge hackle

Note: Many fly tiers recommend adding a short orange-colored throat.

ARTICULATED YELLOW DRAKE FLY NYMPH
(*Ephemera varia*)

Hook:	#10 Aberdeen hook trimmed to 7 mm (abdomen), #16 Tiemco 2488 (thorax)
Thread:	Tan 8/0 Uni-Thread
Tails:	Three natural gray ostrich herl tips
Abdomen:	Tannish yellow Harrop CEN Dubbing and natural light mottled brown turkey quill
Rib:	Fine gold wire
Gills:	Natural gray philoplume and feather-base marabou
Thorax:	Same as abdomen
Wing Case:	Mottled oak Thin Skin and pearl Flashabou coated with five-minute epoxy
Legs:	Natural tan-brown hen pheasant hackle
Tusks:	Tannish yellow goose biot tips

ARTICULATED HEX FLY NYMPH
(*Hexagenia limbata*)

Hook:	#6 Aberdeen hook trimmed to 20 mm (abdomen), #10 Tiemco 2488 (thorax)
Thread:	Camel 8/0 Uni-Thread
Tails:	Three natural gray ostrich herl tips
Abdomen:	Rusty olive Harrop CEN Dubbing and natural dark mottled brown turkey quill
Rib:	Fine gold wire
Gills:	Natural gray philoplume and feather-base marabou
Thorax:	Same as abdomen
Wing Case:	Mottled oak Thin Skin and pearl Flashabou coated with five-minute epoxy
Legs:	Dyed olive hen pheasant hackle
Tusks:	Brown goose biot tips

11

The Hydropsyche Caddis Larva

Beyond sheer numbers, the larva of Hydropsychid caddisflies
have much to recommend them to the angler.

THOMAS AMES, *CADDISFLIES*

The larval imitations of the *Hydropsyche* genus, often referred to as spotted sedges or net-spinning caddis, are important foods for trout. First, this caddis genus enjoys a vast distribution on many streams and rivers across the United States and Europe and can be found in many freestone environments where pollution has impacted less hardy insect larvae such as mayflies and stoneflies. Lastly, the *Hydropsyche* caddis are a free-crawling variety that is always available to the fish year-round. The larvae of many caddis species construct small cases from twigs and small pieces of bark or from sand and stream gravel; *Hydropsyche* caddis larvae on the other hand roam freely about the streambed and construct small silken nets much like spiders do in the crevices between stones to filter the stream currents for the microinvertebrates that they feed upon. As a result, they are often one of the trout's primary food sources, and fish expect to find them among the rubble and stones of the streambed when no other insects are active. Because of this, the Hydropsyche Caddis Larva is the perfect search

The Hydropsyche Caddis Larva is an effective pattern on many streams because of the naturals' wide distribution. On streams with good caddis populations this is often my favorite search pattern, and flies both with and without beads are useful. JAY NICHOLS

Beadhead variations of the pattern are very effective and should be tied on size 14 through 18 curved hooks. The natural larvae always have some degree of curvature in their bodies, particularly when they become dislodged and drift in the current. JAY NICHOLS

The thick and branchlike gills on caddis larvae make a spiky dubbing material like natural hare's mask a perfect choice when picked and brushed out along the underside of the fly to imitate them. JAY NICHOLS

pattern to fish when there are no obvious caddisfly hatches.

The small larvae range in size from 8 to 13 millimeters and are usually a dirty tannish gray in color with a darker head and thorax area. The body is heavily segmented and thickly gilled on the underside for the entire length of its abdomen. The legs are short and feeble compared with many aquatic insect larvae. The simple pattern presented here was developed years ago by English fly tier Oliver Edwards; I've modified it somewhat over the years. Several physical features of these nymphs are immediately apparent and distinctively different in appearance from many of the other macroinvertebrates found in our streams. The larva has a large plumose-looking appendage on the end of its abdomen that it uses to anchor itself securely to its net and in inching its way across the streambed. The other obvious physical feature is the profile of the larva. Once these caddis larvae lose the security of their grip on something solid they immediately curl in a defensive posture until touching the stream bottom again. Even at rest the larvae seldom straighten themselves and always have a curvature to

A rainbow that fell for a Beadhead Hydropsyche Larva.

their bodies. In developing an effective imitation of the *Hydropsyche* caddis it is critical to incorporate these two features into the design. Such physical features become visual aids or triggers to a feeding trout. For my patterns I prefer the curved Daiichi 1130 or 1120 hook, which duplicates this curved profile nicely, yet still has good hooking ability compared with many of the designs available from other hook manufacturers.

To imitate the distinctive tail tuft of the naturals, the best material I've found is the base down of a bird feather or the after shaft or philoplume found on most land-dwelling birds like pheasants, partridges, or grouse. This material is often more of a bluish gray in color, and I prefer the warmer tannish gray shade of the body feathers from female pheasants. The abdominal segments of the larva are also heavily gilled on the underside. To imitate this I use a spiky dubbing blend made from the English hare's mask and add about 10 percent Z-Lon fibers, cut to about ¼ inch in length, to give it additional sparkle. After completing the fly I use a dubbing needle to pick out the guard hairs for the entire length of the fly's underside. After this I take the small brush with a

A Hydropsyche larva. These larvae, a net-spinning variety, do not build a protective case. Note the prominent appendages tipped with tiny claws on the tip of the larva's abdomen— known as prolegs, they are used to anchor the larva to streambed stones—and the thick branchlike gill structures on the body's underside. Both prominent features should be incorporated into the nymph imitation.

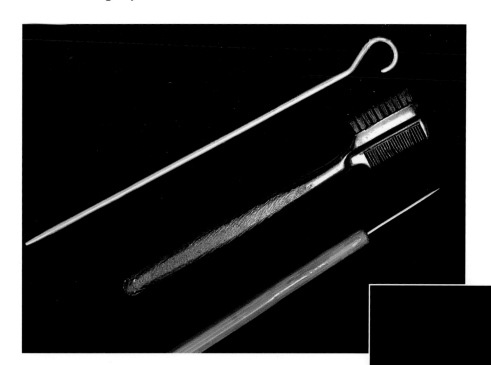

For a dubbing brush, I use a small moustache comb/brush combination that can be found at any pharmacy. The comb side is useful to remove fuzz from deer and other kinds of animal hair. A small piece of Velcro hook-side material on the handle works great to tease out a dubbed body on a nymph or scud pattern. A shepherd's hook is invaluable for creating dubbing loops and for twisting other materials like peacock herls together with thread to reinforce them.

piece of Velcro hook-side material attached to it and comb these picked-out fibers downward, which really does a good job of duplicating the gills as well as the legs of the nymph.

Over the years the Hydropsyche Larva has become one of my favorite nymphs, and my fly boxes always contain a number of them in sizes 14 to 18 tied with and without beads. When you can see the subsurface flashes of trout feeding on nymphs on the streambed or when there is not any obvious feeding activity, this nymph is always a good search pattern to begin with, either by itself or fished in a dropper rig. The pattern has accounted for many successful days over the years and is often the first fly pattern I reach for when there is no obvious hatching activity and the stream I'm on has good caddis populations.

TYING THE HYDROPSYCHE CADDIS LARVA

HYDROPSYCHE CADDIS LARVA

Hook:	#14-18 Daiichi 1120 or 1130
Thread:	Tan 8/0 Uni-Thread
Tail:	Tuft of tannish gray feather-base marabou fibers or philoplumes
Body:	Grayish tan hare's mask dubbing blended with about 10 percent amber and brown Z-Lon
Overback:	Dark brown mottled turkey-tail strip
Rib:	Fine gold wire
Head:	Top of head and first two segments behind it colored with French gray Prismacolor marker

Note: Pick out the underside of the fly with a dubbing needle and brush it with Velcro to simulate the nymph's gills and legs. You can add a gold bead (³⁄₃₂" for size 14, ⁵⁄₆₄" for size 16, and ¹⁄₁₆" for size 18 flies).

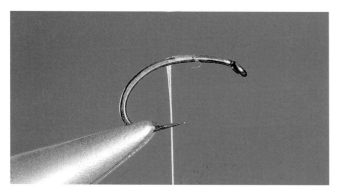

1. Clamp a heavy-wire curved hook in the vise and attach tan 8/0 thread at the midpoint. Wrap the tying thread back toward the hook bend, stopping at a point above and just slightly beyond the end of the barb.

2. Select a marabou-like feather from a hen pheasant skin and strip off the fibers from the feather's base. The best feathers will be on the underside of the bird close to the tail. Separate a group of approximately 12 to 15 fibers and strip them from the feather.

3. Tie in the clump of marabou fibers and trim off the butts. Do not trim the marabou to length.

4. Separate four or five fibers from the turkey tail and cut them from the quill. Trim half an inch from the tips of the fibers.

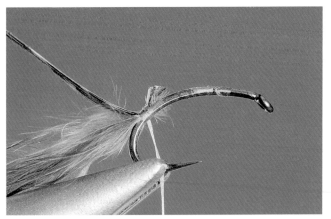

5. Tie in the tips of the turkey-tail fibers flat on top of the hook shank with the dull side facing up.

6. Wrap the tying thread forward to the center of the hook and tie in a piece of fine gold wire on the underside of the hook, wrapping back to the point where the turkey and tail are tied in.

7. Apply a mixture of natural hare's mask dubbing and 10 percent brown and amber Z-Lon fibers.

8. Dub a fairly even body, finishing with enough space remaining to make a small head.

9. Pull the turkey strip forward with your right hand over the back of the fly so that the strip contacts the back for the first half and hold it there. Begin to rib over the turkey strip and take even turns so that the back is centered.

10. As you wrap forward lower the turkey strip with your right hand to make it easier to keep the strip centered on the top of the body.

11. Tie off both the turkey strip and rib with a few firm turns of thread. Break off the ribbing wire.

12. Trim the turkey strip closely.

13. Build a small head with tying thread. Whip-finish.

14. Snip the tying thread and trim the tail to length.

15. The tail should be approximately one-fourth the body length.

16. Use the dubbing needle to pick out the dubbing fibers between the ribbing wire along the underside of the fly body to create the gills and legs. Pick out the body along its entire length.

17. Brush the teased-out fibers downward with the Velcro tool.

18. The body should be shaggy on the underside when finished.

19. Use a French gray permanent marker to darken the head and the overback for the first two segments. The tail tuft of the nymph is an important characteristic. Using spiky dubbing material makes the imitation of the thick gill structures and legs simple yet effective, and using a curved hook strongly presents the profile of a caddis larva and its distinctive curled posture when caught in the drift.

BEAD-HEAD HYDROPSYCHE

Hook: #14-18 Daiichi 1120 or 1130
Bead: Gold Cyclops or tungsten
Thread: Tan 8/0 Uni-Thread
Tail: Tuft of tannish gray feather-base marabou fibers or philoplumes
Body: Grayish tan hare's mask dubbing blended with about 10 percent amber and brown Z-Lon
Overback: Dark brown mottled turkey-tail strip
Rib: Fine gold wire
Head: Top of head and first two segments behind it colored with French gray Prismacolor marker

12

The Swimming Caddis Pupa

Once a hatch is in progress most feeding will initially be on the pupal form of the caddis—an opportunity for some very exciting fishing.

LARRY SOLOMON AND ERIC LEISER, *THE CADDIS AND THE ANGLER*

*U*nlike the unhurried feeding patterns of stream trout to food forms like midges, mayfly spinners, or beetles, the rise of trout to emerging caddis is usually a fast-paced, splashy affair. The speed of the trout's feeding activity is always directly related to the speed of its prey, and no insect species or stage comes close to duplicating the violent rises of trout when they are feeding on swimming or hatching caddis pupae except perhaps some of the fast-swimming mayfly nymphs such as the *Isonychia* and *Ephemera* species. As fishermen, most of us feel inclined to switch from a nymph pattern to a dry adult

imitation as soon as we begin to see regular surface feeding activity, but it often pays to scrutinize the actual rise-forms of the fish before changing our approach. Admittedly I often make this switch because like many others, I really enjoy catching fish on the surface. In fishing many aquatic insect hatches, however, the patient fisherman who is willing to stay with a subsurface pattern can often have amazing results.

Many of the rises we see on the surface are indeed made by trout feeding on hatched insects, but quite often if we really look closer, the fish are only breaking the

Steve Spurgeon swims a caddis pupa pattern on the Savage River in western Maryland.

water as they take something just below the surface or an insect caught in the surface film while hatching. At times the clue is something minimal and hard to detect, but a trout taking an insect on the surface of the water leaves a small bubble in the ring of its rise most of the time, expelling air through its gills as it closes its mouth. A trout that has only disturbed the surface while taking something just below the film of the water will not. Sometimes the clue is more bold and obviously displayed when fish flat-out refuse the adult patterns. When this happens during a caddis hatch, it is usually because the fish are keying on rising pupae rather than hatched adults. This is often true for trout of all sizes, and larger fish often prefer to feed subsurface on swimming pupae rather than expose themselves to predators by rising to the surface.

The caddisfly's life cycle is a true metamorphic process with a larval stage, a pupation stage, and a winged adult fly. Mayflies and stoneflies do not undergo pupation and instead make the transformation from the larval stage straight to a winged adult. Caddis spend their larval stages in a variety of ways. Some species such as those of the genuses *Brachycentrus* and *Glossosoma* construct small cases from sand, gravel, bark, and vegetable matter found on the stream bottom and bonded together to create a protective case for the larvae to live in. The cases themselves may be attached to the stones of the streambed where the caddis remains until pupation is completed, and some caddis species will move about the streambed, pulling their case homes along with them. Other species such as the bright green larvae of the genuses *Rhyacophila* and the net-building *Hydropsyche* crawl about on the streambed free of any type of casing. At the time of pupation the larvae of the case-building varieties will enclose the case they live in. Free-crawling caddis larvae will seal themselves in a silken chrysalis-like capsule in the same manner as a butterfly or construct a case to undergo the transformation. These cases will usually be attached to stones on the streambed with silk. The actual process of pupation usually

takes only a few weeks to accomplish, and once it is completed the pupa will exit the case.

The deeply segmented caddis larva looks and moves like a worm, extending and contracting its body in the course of moving about. The leg structures are often short yet thick as they are only needed to crawl about and hold position on the streambed. Once the pupation is complete, the long wormlike larva transforms into a compressed pupa with a robust body that lacks the larva's well-defined segmentation. The legs of the pupa stage are long, extending almost to the end of the abdomen, and paddlelike in shape, which helps the pupa to swim quickly to the surface with oarlike swimming strokes. Wing cases, 50 to 75 percent of the length of the body, extend at a slight downward angle along the sides of the body. The wing cases hug tight against the body of the pupa and are dark in color. The pupa spends a short time in this state and makes its way toward the surface to hatch into an adult insect. The caddis pupa at the time of emergence takes on a shiny or sparkly quality as it generates gases within the outer skin of its body that help to buoy it to the surface to hatch and also assist in releasing the pupa's outer layer of skin from the inner skin of the mature adult insect. These gases also help split the skin's outer casing, which makes it easier for the adult to emerge. Building this bright, sparkly appearance into our fly patterns is critical.

Caddis imitations have been around for many years and the most effective ones have found a way to create this image for the fish. The soft-hackled flies of Yorkshire, England, are great imitations of emerging caddis pupae and have been in use for well over 100 years. The key to the success of these flies lies in the way that these patterns trap a small air bubble behind the thin collar of soft bird hackles used to dress them, like partridge, grouse, plover, and starling. Capturing this small air bubble imitates well the sparkling appearance of a hatching pupa, and the soft fibers of the hackle collar are free to move about to imitate nicely the movements of the natural insects legs. Classic soft-hackled patterns like the Partridge and Green and Grouse and Green are still great patterns to imitate caddis pupae. Gary LaFontaine revolutionized subsurface caddis imitations and fishing techniques with the release of *Caddisflies* in 1987. The patterns presented in this landmark book have become the standard for fishermen. His Sparkle Pupa is simple to make and effective as a fishing tool due to the way the materials simulate this glistening quality of the actual pupa. LaFontaine developed a unique method for creating a pupa using a thinly dubbed body core veiled by sparkly Antron. This yarn is tied in before the abdomen of the fly is dubbed, pulled forward loosely over the body core, and then tied down in front of the body to create a

A selection of swimming-caddis pupae imitations. JAY NICHOLS

Above: Much of the feeding during a caddisfly hatch takes place subsurface, and many of the rises we see are false rises made by trout taking pupae just below the surface. It is important to study riseforms closely during these hatches. BARRY AND CATHY BECK

A nice rainbow trout. Many larger fish choose to feed on emergent flies rather than adults, which are more difficult to capture.
BARRY AND CATHY BECK

veiled bubble effect with the yarn fibers. Antron, a remarkable trilobal fiber, reflects light much better than a rounded or oval cross-sectioned fiber can.

The caddis pupa imitation I favor is based on René Harrop's Ascending Caddis. While this is an effective pattern, I wanted to add more detail to improve it and have been happy with the results. This modification tries to capitalize on the characteristics of the natural pupa that have proven to be visual triggers to feeding trout. The body is formed from a spiky dubbing with an overback of Darlon or Z-Lon yarn, which is ribbed into place with fine wire. The yarn overback gives a beautiful sheen to the body of the fly, and the ribbing wire enhances the effect while also introducing some defined segmentation. The wing cases on the sides of the pupa's body are a dominant characteristic, and for imitating these I use a dyed flashback film that is soft and durable and imparts some additional sparkle to the fly. For the legs I use a collar of brown Hungarian partridge hackle fibers, which imitate the legs on a traditional soft-hackled wet pattern and provide some movement as the fly is twitched during its drift. For realism I add two long lemon wood-duck fibers to represent antennae, and the fly is completed with a dubbed head from a brown-colored squirrel dubbing blend.

The Swimming Pupa can be fished with a number of different presentations. The pupa can be fished deep on a swing with motion imparted to suggest a pupa migrating toward the surface to hatch. This presentation is made by first casting across and upstream to achieve a deeper presentation and then allowing the fly to swing at the end of the drift. This is an effective approach, and the fish often take the fly as it completes the drift and starts to swing on a tight line and rise through the water. The Swimming Pupa is also effective fished as a dropper, and I often use one in tandem with a CDC Adult Caddis pattern to keep the fly suspended just below the film when fish are visibly breaking the surface as they pursue the rising pupa. Fish will often take either pattern during a hatch, and the dry pattern serves as an indicator to telegraph a strike to the pupa.

Fortunately for us, caddis pupae are not found in a range of diverse colors, shapes, and sizes like mayfly nymphs. Most of the more commonly found caddis species are colored in a variety of greens, tans, dark grays, and browns, and most of them can be imitated with a small assortment of basic patterns tied in a range of sizes to match them. The patterns in this chapter are some of my favorites and should be modified to match the colors of the natural pupae in the streams you fish.

TYING THE SWIMMING PUPA (TAN-GRAY)

SWIMMING CADDIS PUPA (Tan-Gray)
(Hydropsyche, Helicopsyche spp., Glossosoma spp.)

Hook:	#16-20 Tiemco 206BL
Thread:	Camel 8/0 Uni-Thread
Abdomen:	Natural hare's mask dubbing mixed with 10 percent amber and brown Z-Lon fibers chopped short, with tan Z-Lon or Darlon pulled over the top
Rib:	Gold Ultra Wire (extra small)
Wing cases:	Black-dyed flashback film strip (Hareline)
Legs:	Brown Hungarian partridge fibers
Antennae:	Two wood-duck flank fibers
Head:	Brown SLF Squirrel Dubbing

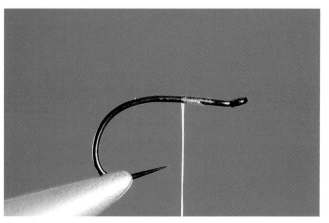

1. Clamp a Tiemco 206BL hook in the vise and attach camel 8/0 thread just behind the hook eye.

3. Wrap the tying thread forward to the center of the hook and tie in a length of fine gold wire on the underside of the hook. Wrap back toward the bend, securing the wire as you go.

2. Wrap the tying thread back toward the hook bend, stopping approximately one-fourth of the way around the hook bend. Cut a section of tan Darlon and tie it in, leaving a short length protruding backward.

4. Apply the dubbing and build an even body, stopping just under one-fourth of the way from the hook eye.

5. Pull the yarn forward over the back of the fly with your right hand so that the yarn contacts the first half of the back. With even turns, wrap over the yarn with the gold wire. Take care to center the yarn on the back of the fly.

6. Tie off the yarn and wire.

7. Break off the ribbing wire and cut off the surplus yarn. Trim the yarn short at the rear of the body so that it is approximately one-eighth the length of the fly's body.

8. Cut a strip of black flashback film so that it is about 1½ inches long and equivalent to ½ the hook gap in width. Fold the strip lengthwise and round the tips of the strip to form the wing cases.

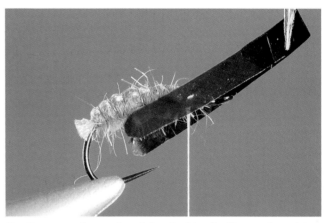

9. Separate the ends of the flashback film and position the strip so that it straddles the fly. The strips should sit low and flat on each side of the body and angle downward slightly.

10. Slide the wing cases back until they are approximately three-fourths the length of the body. With the thumb and forefinger of your left hand, pinch the wing cases against the sides of the body. Take one complete turn of thread loosely around the wing cases before pulling it tight in an upward direction.

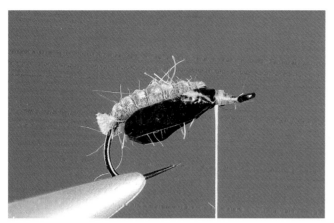

11. Take a few more firm turns of thread and trim off the surplus wing-case material.

12. Select a brown partridge hackle and cut a V notch in the feather to remove the tip. Bring the notched feather flat to the front of the fly so that it straddles the body. Bring the hackle back until the tips of the fibers reach the end of the body. Fold the hackle fibers downward so that they are flat against each side of the body and held in this position with your left thumb and forefinger. Take one complete turn of tying thread loosely around the partridge hackle and pull the thread tight in an upward direction. The hackle fibers should now be distributed cvenly around the fly. Take several firm turns of thread to anchor the hackle and trim off the surplus.

13. Select two fairly straight lemon wood-duck fibers and hold them in position so that they are on each side of the body and angle back over it to form the antennae. The fibers should extend just past the fly's body. Pinch the fibers in this position with your left thumb and forefinger and secure them in place.

14. Trim off the excess wood-duck fibers and dub a head of brown SLF Squirrel Dubbing. Whip-finish and cut off the tying thread, and the tan-gray Swimming Caddis Pupa is complete. This swimming caddis, which captures the sparkling quality of an emergent pupa with the use of reflective materials in the abdomen and the wing cases, incorporates some of the important qualities and techniques found in the effective soft-hackle wet flies of the nineteenth and twentieth centuries.

SWIMMING PUPA (Emerald Green)
(*Rhyacophila, Cheumatopsyche* spp.)

Hook: #14–20 Tiemco 206BL
Thread: Camel 8/0 Uni-Thread
Abdomen: Pale green Life Cycle dubbing and light green Darlon
Rib: Gold Ultra Wire (extra small)
Wing cases: Black-dyed flashback film strip (Hareline)
Legs: Brown Hungarian partridge fibers
Antennae: Two wood-duck flank fibers
Head: Brown SLF Squirrel Dubbing

SWIMMING PUPA (Apple Green)
(*Rhyacophila, Brachycentrus* spp.)

Hook: #14–20 Tiemco 206BL
Thread: Camel 8/0 Uni-Thread
Abdomen: Caddis green Harrop CEN Dubbing and fluorescent green Darlon
Rib: Gold Ultra Wire (extra small)
Wing cases: Black-dyed flashback film strip (Hareline)
Legs: Brown Hungarian partridge fibers
Antennae: Two wood-duck flank fibers
Head: Brown SLF Squirrel Dubbing

SWIMMING PUPA (Dark Gray)
(*Psilotreta* spp.)

Hook: #16–20 Tiemco 206BL
Thread: Iron gray 8/0 Uni-Thread
Abdomen: Dark gray Sow-Scud Dubbing and dark dun Darlon
Rib: Gold Ultra Wire (extra small)
Wing cases: Black-dyed flashback film strip (Hareline)
Legs: Brown Hungarian partridge fibers
Antennae: Two wood-duck flank fibers
Head: Dark brown SLF Squirrel Dubbing

SWIMMING PUPA (Great Red Sedge) (*Pycnopsyche* spp.)

Hook:	#10–12 Tiemco 206BL
Thread:	Rusty brown 8/0 Uni-Thread
Abdomen:	Rust Harrop CEN Dubbing and amber Darlon
Rib:	Gold Ultra Wire (extra small)
Wing Cases:	Black-dyed flashback film strip (Hareline)
Legs:	Brown Hungarian partridge fibers
Antennae:	Two wood-duck flank fibers
Head:	Brown SLF Squirrel Dubbing

13

The CDC Adult Caddis

Let us now define design as the way materials are chosen and assembled in order to achieve a desired structural task. That task is to control behavior above all.

DATUS PROPER, *WHAT THE TROUT SAID*

In the July 1991 issue of *Fly Fisherman,* René Harrop launched a fly-tying revolution of sorts by introducing American anglers to the cul-de-canard (CDC) feathers found on most waterfowl species. Previously most dry flies had floated with the support of stiff rooster hackles or hollow deer or elk hair. The marabou-like structure of the CDC feathers and their barbules captures air within the fibers, which are also naturally buoyant from the oils secreted by the preening gland of the ducks and geese that the feathers are taken from. Harrop devel-

oped a host of imitations for the difficult rainbows of the Henry's Fork of the Snake in Idaho, where the selective fish challenge even the most accomplished fishermen.

For several years, the purist in me was reluctant to experiment with these peculiar feathers. The vague silhouettes of patterns tied with CDC seemed like they would be ineffective in imitating the well-defined features of some insects. How could they be successful with selective fish? The patterns I started to see in the local shops looked more like small tufts of fluff and thistledown than

The adult caddisfly plays a huge role on most trout streams, being able to tolerate degraded water conditions that more sensitive insects such as mayflies and stoneflies cannot. JAY NICHOLS

The orange-colored Pycnopsyche *or October Caddis hatches in September and October and is the largest caddis species found in the east.*

Below: The Grannom Caddis, also known as the Mother's Day Caddis or Shad Fly, is a member of the Brachycentrus *genus, which consists of a number of species including* lateralis, solomoni, *and* numerosus *among others. Grannoms, one of the first caddis species to emerge each spring, can hatch in astonishing numbers that attract many rising trout.*

The Hydropsyche *caddis or Speckled Sedge is one of the most widely distributed species in the eastern United States.*

practical fly imitations. But, over time, I finally abandoned my traditional streak and began experimenting with CDC to solve the difficult puzzle of the caddis feeders along Tulpehocken Creek.

Some of my own early caddisfly imitations employed a host of different animal hairs for the wing material including groundhog, blesbok, whitetail deer, elk, and mink hair bundles in the already proven down-wing styles of Larry Solomon and Eric Leiser. For several years I experimented with synthetic films, even using carefully folded and trimmed-down wings of Swiss Straw to create a well-defined caddisfly imitation. These incredibly realistic patterns, however, were inconsistent in attracting fish.

When I overcame my disdain for CDC, my caddis patterns finally succeeded. Adult caddis imitations using rooster hackles fail on selective fish in calmer waters primarily due to the way they float on the water. The natural sits close to the water with much of the body in

contact with the film, especially in the case of ovipositing and spent flies. The light patterns created by the full or partially hackled flies do not create the correct light pattern due to their high floating characteristics. The tough fish of the Tully demanded flies that were more exacting.

The simple adult CDC caddis I eventually settled on is really nothing spectacular in its appearance, but it is constructed differently than other caddis patterns. Sparsely tied CDC flies may look good in fly shop bins, but there generally is not enough CDC on them to float the fly well. Yet, if you did put a lot of CDC on the fly, customers would not tolerate the crude, oversize heads of the flies.

To solve this problem, I borrowed one of Jack Gartside's techniques: he initially tied the materials in the fly's construction so that they pointed forward over the hook eye and then reversed and tied them back to create a clean head. Jack's technique created a slick grasshopper pattern that did not obstruct the hook eye with the

The CDC Adult Caddis is an effective fly for difficult conditions and is simple to tie. Tying the material in a reversed or bullet-head pattern easily manages the bulky CDC and clears the hook eye. JAY NICHOLS

Caddisflies sit close to the stream surface with the wings folded back in a tent-like position. Adult caddis move much more than mayflies do when drifting on the water, making soft CDC fibers a great material to imitate the wings. JAY NICHOLS

trimmed butts of the winging material. Tying CDC on the fly in this manner allowed me to not only use enough material to float the flies well but also to fashion a neat head so that nothing blocks your fine tippet as you try to thread it through the hook eye in the fading light of evening.

In addition to CDC's floatability, the success of this pattern is due to the inherent movement of the fibers. Whether a hatching fly that hopscotches and skitters across the surface or an egg-laying female that constantly twitches, caddis adults never stay still, which creates a unique presentation challenge. In this pattern, the heavily fibered wing moves about in the available air currents and the angle of the fibers realistically simulates a caddisfly trying to fly away or lay its eggs. I often use as many as four CDC feathers to wing a size 18 fly. I think the bulky wing creates a better illusion than a sparsely dressed one, and the fly often becomes less effective when the CDC

fibers begin to absorb moisture and start to mat up, reducing the fly's silhouette.

The body of this simple dry fly is best tied with a slightly "spiky" dubbing blend that helps to create the illusion of legs by the small to moderate percentage of guard hair in the mix. My favorite commercial blend is the Life Cycle dubbing blends by Wapsi in the popular caddis colors, especially the green and tan shades. The blends of natural and synthetic fibers have a good sheen without being overly glitzy, and the colors are accurate when the dubbing material gets wet. I make my own blend for the *Hydropsyche* caddis by mixing English hare's mask fur from the cheek and forehead regions of the mask with about 10 percent amber and medium brown Z-Lon chopped about one-quarter inch long and mixed in a dubbing blender to create a buggy grayish tan mixture.

When I first began to demonstrate the CDC Adult Caddis at shows and tying classes, I did it with reserva-

Cul-de-Canard

"CDC" is the common term used in reference to cul-de-canard plumes found on most waterfowl species. In the middle of the backs of ducks and geese, close to the root of the tail, is the uropygial gland, which secretes preening oil that these birds use to waterproof their feathers. Waterfowl often rub their bills in this area of their backs and then using their bills to distribute this oil over the body and wing feathers. The unique structure and physical properties of the feathers that surround this gland have opened a whole new world of possibilities in imitative fly tying. The feathers' soft texture and fine fibers covered with tiny barbules or microbarbs make them look fuzzy and full, like miniature marabou

CDC feathers can be used to make high-floating dry flies due to the fiber structure that captures air bubbles to create floatation, while their fine texture moves to help create the illusion of life.

plumes. These tiny barbules allow the fibers to trap and hold tiny bubbles of air captive within them, permitting fly tiers to create flies with good floatation, but even more importantly to create flies with the illusion of life. Live insects at most points of their life cycles are in a state of constant movement: swimming to the surface to emerge, wriggling to free themselves from the nymphal shuck, and working their wings in an effort to dry them and gain the air. This ability to better imitate something with life and vitality is oftentimes the critical difference between failure and success in clear, placid waters.

My first exposure to these plumes came from an article in *Fly Fisherman* magazine by René Harrop in 1991. I was skeptical because the patterns appeared to be entirely too vague and nondescript compared to the no-hackle patterns of Swisher and Richards, the trimmed feather duns of Chauncy Lively and Poul Jorgensen, and the spent spinner wings fashioned from hen-hackle tips popular through the 1970s and '80s. Tony Gehman of Tulpehocken Creek Outfitters showed me the patterns he was using that incorporated CDC material to imitate wings on the small caddisflies and mayflies for Tulpehocken Creek, and I dismissed them as well and continued with the more defined school of thought. I had spent most of a year tying and testing a variety of synthetic films trimmed to shape to better imitate adult caddisflies and was having limited success with these flies despite the well-defined silhouettes that looked exact in appearance. Fish would immediately move toward these patterns when presented them, but they refused the patterns after closer inspection. Several years later after a lot of frustration I swallowed my pride and purchased several bags of CDC feathers to experiment with. I will not

tion. Like a housewife who jealously guards her culinary secrets from even her closest friends and family members, I didn't want to let others in on what was working out so wonderfully for me. While I do enjoy crafting highly detailed fly patterns, there's a great level of satisfaction with developing a simple solution to a difficult fishing problem. The CDC Adult Caddis is my simplest solution to date for difficult fish. A good selection of these flies in body colors of various shades of grayish brown, tan, olive, apple green, spruce green, cinnamon, and black in sizes ranging from #14 to #24 will suffice for nearly any caddis you are likely to encounter.

The hook is also an important ingredient in the fly. Improvements in hook design over the past 15 years have opened doors to crafting patterns that are more exacting

in profile and proportion to natural insects than ever possible before. The wings on a caddis adult are dramatically longer than the body, which makes an extra-short shank hook useful. My favorite hook for this type of pattern is the light-wire, wide-gap Varivas 988, which unfortunately is not produced anymore. The best replacement for this hook is the Tiemco 2488, which has a slightly heavier wire diameter than the Varivas hook. The heavier wire is good for holding larger fish on stouter tippets and the short shank length makes well-proportioned caddis imitations.

For any CDC pattern to be most effective, rinse the fly thoroughly, press it between the folds of a patch of chamois or amadou to dry it, and treat the fly with a powder floatant. You can also use one of the fly desiccants say that there was an immediate turnaround in my success on the stream, as there was considerable time spent learning how to use the material and how to maximize its potential. The results of my experiments with CDC over the next few years did eventually transform my thinking, my tying, and my effectiveness as a fisherman, and CDC feathers now serve as a foundation in many of my patterns.

To gain the most from CDC, it is important to understand the feathers and be able to choose the right type for the application—not all CDC feathers are the same in terms of usefulness. There are different types of CDC feathers, coming from different spots in proximity to the bird's preening gland. In an article published in *Fly Fisherman* magazine several years ago, Hans Weilenmann presents a great method to identify the various shapes and uses of these unique feathers, grouping them into four feather types. I highly recommend reading this article.

TYPE 1

The fibers of these feathers angle at between 45 and 60 degrees from a well-defined stem. They typically have a slightly rounded tip, and the fibers usually have dense barbules along their entire length. Type 1 feathers work well when bunched together and tied in as post wings on patterns such as the CDC Thorax Duns, Half-and-Half Emergers, and CDC Comparaduns. They are also useful for the larger CDC Adult Caddis patterns.

TYPE 2

The fibers of these feathers run nearly parallel to thin stems. The tips of these plumes are somewhat square at the tip, and the barbs on each fiber are not as dense or heavy as the type 1 feather. These are good feathers for small mayfly dun and adult caddis wings and for making loop wings in some emerger patterns.

TYPE 3

These feathers are often referred to as puffs or oiler puffs. They have no central stem and are similar to blood marabou in structure. Puffs have good barb density and are great floaters, but are small and short in length, which limits them to tiny dun and emerger patterns.

TYPE 4

These are the longest variety of CDC feathers and have a heavier central stem than the other types. The fibers at the tips have little or no microbarbs, but the dense barbs and good usable length of the side fibers make them useful in patterns that trim or strip the side fibers from the stem. Tiers using the strip method often stack several feathers on top of one another to speed the tying process. I use type 4 feathers for the Almost Dun series.

When purchasing CDC, look for feathers that have dense microbarbs along the length of the fibers. CDC feathers will naturally be treated with preen oil, but you must first remove it to dye the feathers. Make sure the feathers have not been damaged during bleaching or overheating from the dyeing process, which can quickly ruin the fiber quality and fishability of your flies by destroying the tiny barbs.

as a drying agent. After drying the fly well, brush a liberal amount of Frog's Fanny on and into the wings. If you do not use Frog's Fanny, you are not getting the most from your CDC flies. After this treatment, your fly will perk up and float like a fresh one out of your fly box.

The pattern is best fished up and across stream, but you should also try a down and across presentation with a few slight twitches as the fly drifts into the fish's view. Because a number of caddis species such as *Hydropsyche* will also swim underwater to deposit their eggs, I also fish the adult pattern with a microshot about six inches up on the leader with a regular upstream dead-drift presentation to imitate an egg-laying caddis. Many times on the stream you will notice caddis landing on your waders, and if you take a moment to watch them, you will often see the adult flies walk down your leg into the water. Once the flies reach the stream bottom or other solid feature and lay their eggs, they will drift back to the surface and fly away. In faster water currents, this upward drift to the surface can cover a considerable distance and fishing an adult pattern as a subsurface presentation is effective.

You can also modify this pattern to imitate an emerger by adding a trailing shuck and fishing it either in the film or under the surface. My favorite variation, the Hatching CDC Caddis, is made by adding a short length of an amber-colored shuck made from Antron, Z-Lon, or Darlon. Z-Lon fibers get my nod as the favorite in this material category due to a slightly higher amount of reflection and crinkly texture.

TYING THE HYDROPSYCHE CDC CADDIS (TAN)

HYDROPSYCHE CDC CADDIS (Tan)

Hook: #16–22 Tiemco 2488
Thread: Tan 8/0 Uni-Thread
Shuck (optional): Amber Z-Lon
Body: English hare's mask dubbing blended with 10 percent amber and brown Z-Lon cut into ¼-inch lengths
Wing: Natural brown CDC

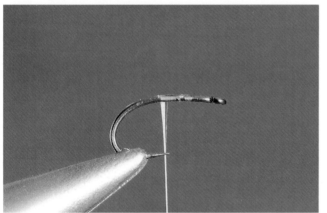

1. Clamp a 2XS, wide-gap dry-fly hook in the vise and attach 8/0 tan thread at the midpoint.

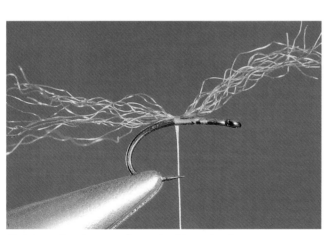

2. To make the Hatching Caddis variation cut a section of amber Z-Lon an inch long and separate 12 to 15 strands. Tie the fibers in at the midpoint of the hook shank, near the center of the fibers. Omit the fibers for the adult variation.

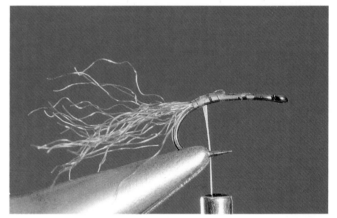

3. Fold the fibers back so that they are doubled and anchor them in place by wrapping back to a point over the end of the hook's barb. Do not trim the shuck to length yet.

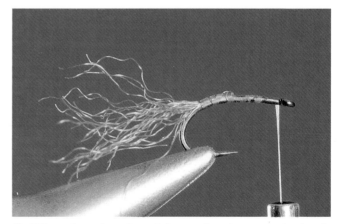

4. Wrap the tying thread forward and stop at the hook eye.

5. Select three natural brown CDC plumes and stack them with the tips aligned. Hold the CDC feather bundle over the hook shank to determine the correct wing length. The wing should be 1¼ to 1½ times the length of the hook shank.

6. Grip the CDC feathers with the thumb and forefinger of your left hand and hold them tightly against the top of the hook shank. Take one loose turn of thread completely around the wings and pull the thread taut. Be sure to keep the CDC fibers on the top of the hook shank. Take several more firm turns of tying thread to secure the wing.

7. Trim the butts of the wings closely and take a few more firm wraps of thread. Wrap the thread to the base of the shuck.

8. Twist dubbing material—a blend of hare's ear and 10 percent amber and brown Z-Lon fibers—tightly on the tying thread.

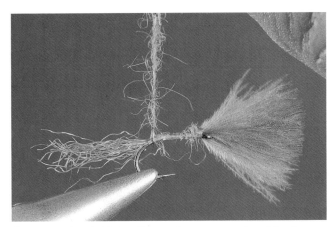

9. Wrap the dubbing forward to create a level body.

10. Dub the fly's body up to the tie-in point of the wing. The body should be even. Wrap the tying thread back toward the bend so that it is one hook eye length behind the wing tie-in point.

11. With your left hand, pull the CDC fibers back over the body tightly. Take a turn of thread around the wing and pull tight and make a second turn to anchor the wing in the final position over the body.

12. The wing is now secured in the final position. Note that the head is small.

13. Bring the tying thread forward between the head of the fly and the hook eye on the underside of the fly.

14. Whip-finish the thread in the gap between the head and the hook eye.

15. Trim the thread closely.

16. Trim the trailing shuck to a length equal to ½ to ¾ the length of the hook shank.

17. The finished Tan Hydropsyche CDC Caddis. Note that this technique, which maximizes the floatation of the fly, makes the fullness of the wing possible. The eye area is also clear and completely unobstructed by the CDC fibers.

CDC CADDIS (Apple Green)

Hook: #14–22 Tiemco 2488
Thread: Tan 8/0 Uni-Thread
Shuck (optional): Amber Z-Lon
Body: Caddis green Life Cycle dubbing
Wing: Natural tan CDC

CDC CADDIS (Emerald)

Hook: #16–22 Tiemco 2488
Thread: Tan 8/0 Uni-Thread
Shuck (optional): Amber Z-Lon
Body: Pale green Life Cycle dubbing
Wing: Natural brown CDC

CDC CADDIS (Cinnamon)

Hook: #16-22 Tiemco 2488
Thread: Rusty brown 8/0 Uni-Thread
Shuck (optional): Amber Z-Lon
Body: Cinnamon caddis Superfine dubbing
Wing: Golden brown CDC

CDC CADDIS (Gray)

Hook: #16-22 Tiemco 2488
Thread: Rusty dun 8/0 Uni-Thread
Shuck (optional): Amber Z-Lon
Body: Ginger Life Cycle dubbing
Wing: Natural dark dun CDC

CDC CADDIS (Black)

Hook: #16-22 Tiemco 2488
Thread: Black 8/0 Uni-Thread
Shuck (optional): Amber Z-Lon
Body: Black Life Cycle dubbing
Wing: Dyed black CDC

CDC CADDIS (Dark Dun)

Hook: #14–18 Tiemco 2488
Thread: Iron dun 8/0 Uni-Thread
Shuck (optional): Amber Z-Lon
Body: Dark gray beaver dubbing
Wing: Natural brown CDC

CDC CADDIS (Grannom)

Hook: #12–14 Tiemco 2488
Thread: Dark brown 8/0 Uni-Thread
Shuck (optional): Amber Z-Lon
Egg Sac: Caddis green CDC trimmed short or a ball of bright green dubbing (for ovipositing adult)
Body: Black Life Cycle dubbing
Wing: Dyed tan CDC

CDC CADDIS (Great Red)

Hook: #10–12 Tiemco 2488
Thread: Rusty brown 8/0 Uni-Thread
Shuck (optional): Amber Z-Lon
Body: Rust Harrop CEN Dubbing
Wing: Golden brown CDC

HATCHING CDC CADDIS (Tan)

Hook:	#14–22 Tiemco 2488
Thread:	Tan 8/0 Uni-Thread
Shuck:	Amber Z-Lon
Body:	English hare's mask dubbing blended with 10 percent amber and brown Z-Lon
Wing:	Natural brown CDC

14

Stonefly Nymphs

Trout feed on the creepers (nymphs) during the entire season
and take them whenever they have an opportunity.

ART FLICK, *NEW STREAMSIDE GUIDE TO NATURALS AND THEIR IMITATIONS*

My fascination with stonefly nymphs began in my early years as a bait fisherman; a stonefly nymph impaled on a light-wire hook and drifted through pockets and pools with a long fly rod was my personal weapon of choice for catching trout. I would often begin the day on the stream overturning flat stones in the shallow riffles to find a few nymphs.

Over time stonefly nymphs gradually became harder and harder to find as suburban sprawl and development began to overtake the rolling hills of southeastern Pennsylvania. Stoneflies require clean water with cooler tem-

peratures and high levels of dissolved oxygen to survive, and they serve as one of the better indicators of a stream's overall health. Like the canary in the coal mine, the stonefly tells the story of a river's water quality. While it is true that we can often find trout without stoneflies being present, we seldom find the stoneflies themselves without also finding trout, provided that an adequate flow of water exists.

Stonefly nymphs are great searching or go-to types of patterns at any time of the season. I usually use one where I know there are populations of them present during the

A Little Yellow Stonefly imitation (Isoperla bilineata) on a hen pheasant skin. The right combination of fiber diameter and naturally colored barring makes these feathers perfect for fashioning the legs on many larger nymphs. JAY NICHOLS

Many stonefly nymphs emerge during the night by crawling onto stones protruding above the waterline. JAY NICHOLS

morning or midday periods when there are no fly hatches occurring. Here in the east, the flies of *Paragnetina capitata* and its cousin *P. immarginata* hatch during the night in June and July by crawling out of the water onto stones. Fishing a nymph imitation early in the morning can be exciting. These flies are effective any other time of the year as well because the nymphs are always present in the stream, and trout, accustomed to seeing them, rarely pass on the opportunity to take one.

Imitating the larger nymphs, which can often run from ½ to 2½ inches in length or more, and the robust features and details in these flies—multiple wing cases, heavily defined abdominal segmentation, dramatic leg structures, and a flattened profile—open the door to a wealth of creative approaches and interpretations to effective imitation.

While today's fly tier can duplicate a wide selection of existing fly patterns of varying degrees of difficulty and complexity from very basic to highly realistic, the pattern that I use with a high level of success is in the middle of these extremes. It is not difficult to tie but it looks realistic enough to get a great reception by the fish.

I've always wanted my flies to appear as lifelike as possible without creating a fly that is too static or stiff to be a fishable imitation, or too labor intensive to be practical. I need to be content with the end result while making flies that my customers can afford.

My personal experimentation of many years has focused on creating distinct differences in the dorsal and ventral surfaces and well-defined wing cases and pronotum in the finished fly. The fly also needs to be somewhat soft to the touch and it needs to move, which is difficult to impart in a fly. Often achieving detail requires reinforcing materials with lacquer or fixatives to preserve the desired shape, whether that be a wing case or legs. The end effect is a stiff and static fly that the fish usually rejects as soon as it touches it. The early stoneflies I tied used mottled turkey-tail or wing-quill sections treated with a clear fixative to keep them from splitting when tied in and folded for an overback or as wing cases. While these flies looked great and fished well, they were not durable. The turkey-quill strips folded to represent wing cases quickly split apart after a fish or two chewed them.

Stoneflies thrive in streams with good water quality and high levels of dissolved oxygen. Deep riffles such as this on Slate Run are perfect runs for drifting a stonefly pattern on the stream bottom. BARRY AND CATHY BECK

Wapsi's Thin Skin is a vinyl film produced in a number of useful colors and several mottled patterns. The material comes on a heavy paper cardstock backing that allows it to be easily and precisely cut to any shape you choose. One side of the film has a somewhat shiny finish while the other is more matte. The semitranslucent material allows any color underneath it to penetrate and create some interesting effects. The material allows you to pull, fold, or stretch it and isn't as frail as more traditional feather strips. The stonefly nymph also differs from many other larval forms: it has a wide, flattened head, which traditional tying methods do not capture well. Folding a strip over the dubbed fly head in reverse creates a more realistic finished fly and keeps the hook eye area free of tying material.

The last significant effect to reproduce is the overall flattened profile of the nymph's abdomen and thorax. To gain the profile of the natural nymph, construct a foundation before dressing the fly. The simple and clever tech-

A nice Penns Creek brown that fell for a deep-drifted stonefly nymph pattern. STEVE SPURGEON

nique of the late Montana fly tier George Grant secured two brass pleating pins, one on each side of the hook shank, with tying thread. I use sections of telecommunication wire with the plastic insulation left intact. Most telephone wire is constructed of four or more conductors

Above: The strategy of fishing stonefly nymphs deep in likely looking pools and drift lanes often pays off well. They are excellent search patterns when no insects are actively hatching.
BARRY AND CATHY BECK

A large Pteronarcys *stonefly nymph. Many stoneflies spend up to two years as a larva before emergence and are an important part of the trout's diet.* JAY NICHOLS

*A large Golden Stonefly nymph (*Agnetina capitata*) presents a husky profile to the trout. The size of many stoneflies presents an opportunity to be creative in designing imitations.*

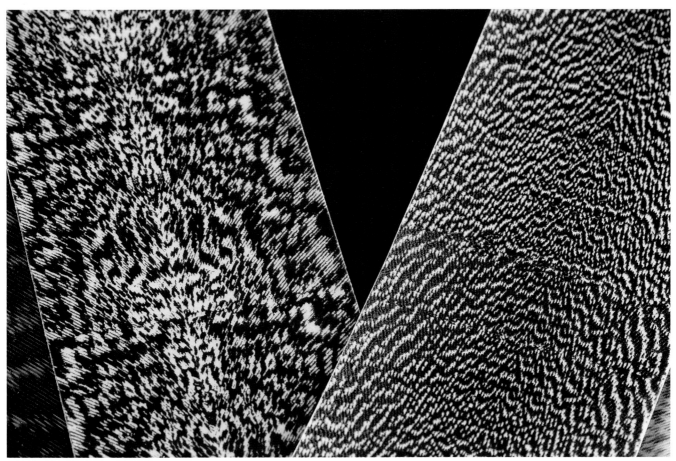

Wapsi's Thin Skin is a thin vinyl sheeting material available in a number of solid colors and printed patterns. In the past, most nymph wing cases were made from strips of wing or tail quills treated with reinforcement such as vinyl cement. These wing cases often split or were easily destroyed by fish. Thin Skin makes a more durable replacement for feather quill sections and looks great when it is overcoated with epoxy to create the humped effect of a mature nymph's wing case. JAY NICHOLS

inside a vinyl jacket, and a section of a foot or two will last the average tier a lifetime. Lash the phone wire sections securely on either side of the hook shank from just forward of the bend to a point just forward of the midpoint of the hook shank. Wind the remaining thorax section with lead wire. After applying both wire types and securing with working thread, flatten both areas with a pair of smooth jawed pliers and then coat the top and bottom with Zap-A-Gap glue. I find the most efficient method is to build a number of these underbodies at a sitting and then put them into boxes labeled by size for future use. I keep a block of foam on my tying bench to hold the fly underbodies, construct a dozen or so, and then coat all of them at the same time. For the smaller imitations such as the *Isoperla* and *Capnia* patterns, I use a finer material for the foundations; for size 12 and smaller flies, .012-inch leader material lashed to the sides of the hook shank works well.

An old Indian adage says that the best way to eat an elephant is "one bite at a time," and the same sentiment

works well when you are tying more complex fly patterns. After making a number of underbodies or foundations, I save a fair amount of time by completing the fly into two separate steps. The first step is to dress the abdomens of a number of nymphs by applying the tails, dubbing the abdomens, and adding the overbody film and ribbing. After completing this step, tie the thread off and return the partially completed nymphs to the foam block until you have all of the abdomens completed. Next I dress the thorax section of each fly by dubbing the thorax sections, adding leg sections, folding the wing cases, and then finishing out the remainder of the fly. Using these production techniques to tie this somewhat involved nymph pattern increases your efficiency at the bench and improves the consistency of your finished flies.

You can easily use this pattern to match any stonefly species by varying the color of the dubbing and the goose biot tails and antennae. The following patterns are my favorites to match the nymphs of most common eastern species.

TYING THE STONEFLY NYMPH (PERLA)

PERLA
(*Agnetina capitata*)

Hook:	#6-8 Tiemco 200
Thread:	Tan 8/0 Uni-Thread
Tails:	Tan goose biots overcolored with dark brown Prismacolor marker
Abdomen:	Creamy yellow Awesome Possum
Rib:	Dark brown D-Rib
Thorax:	Same as abdomen
Legs:	Hen ring-necked pheasant back feather
Wing Cases:	Mottled oak Thin Skin
Head:	Same as abdomen
Antennae:	Same as tails

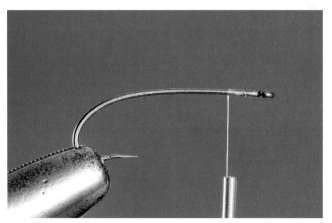

1. Clamp a 3XL nymph hook in the vise and attach tan 8/0 thread immediately behind the hook eye.

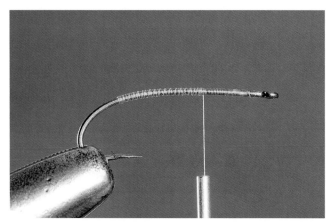

2. Form a thread base by advancing the tying thread toward the hook bend, stopping at a point over the end of the barb. Wrap the thread forward again, stopping ⅓ of the hook length from the eye.

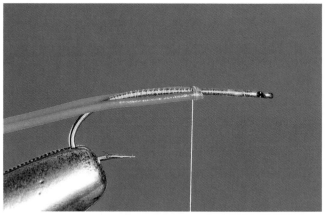

3. To form the underbody double a length of wire and lash the ends on the sides of the hook shank.

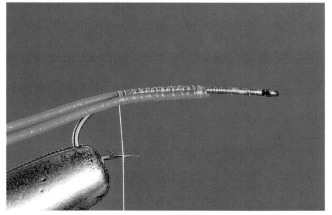

4. Holding the end of the wire taut with your left hand, secure the wire along the sides as you wind back toward the bend. Stop just short of the end of the thread base.

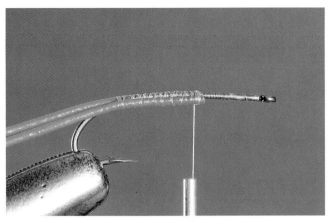

5. Wrap the thread forward to the end of the wire and stop.

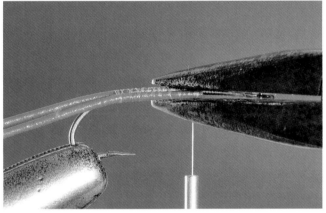

6. Using needle-nose pliers or hemostats with smooth jaws, flatten the wire so that it is straight along both sides of the hook shank.

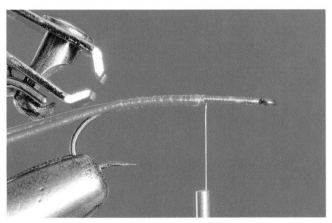

7. Cut the butts of the wire closely with fingernail clippers. The wire trimmed to length should be just short of the point above the end of the hook barb.

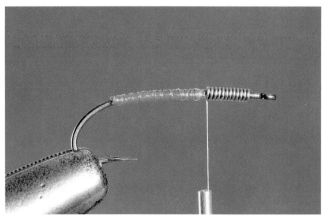

8. Wrap lead wire over the thorax area of the hook, leaving ample space for the head.

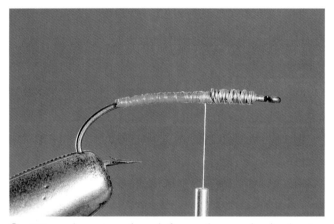

9. Wrap the tying thread forward over the lead wire, then back just past it.

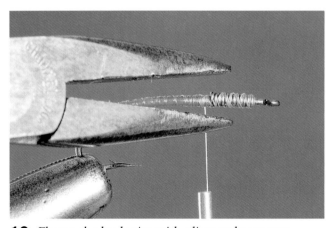

10. Flatten the lead wire with pliers or hemostats.

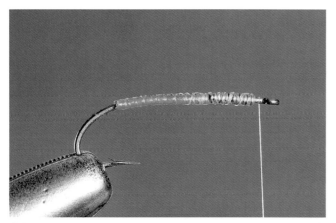

11. Wrap over the lead wire again, stopping at the hook eye.

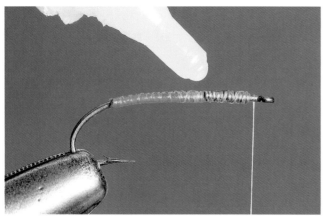

12. Apply Zap-A-Gap glue to the underbody.

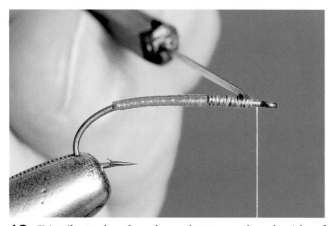

13. Distribute the glue along the top and underside of the underbody with your dubbing needle. Make sure the wraps are well coated.

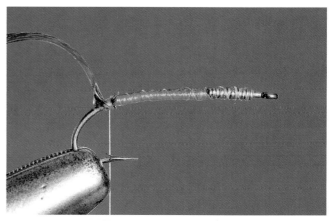

14. Cut a strip of Thin Skin about ⅔ the width of the hook gap with a paper cutter or craft shears. Cut the strip across the end of the sheet. Wrap the tying thread back toward the hook bend and stop just past the ends of the underbody. Tie in the Thin Skin strip by the end with the shiny side facing upward and the strip pointing back beyond the hook bend. Hold the strip flat against the top of the hook and take a loose turn of thread around it. Pull the thread tight to pinch the width of the strip down and keep it flat.

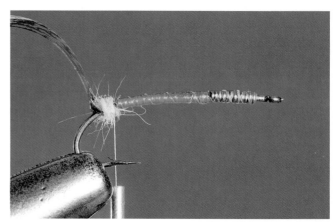

15. Apply creamy yellow Awesome Possum Dubbing to the thread and form a small ball on the hook to cover the tie-in of the back strip. The dubbing should be the same diameter as or slightly larger than the underbody.

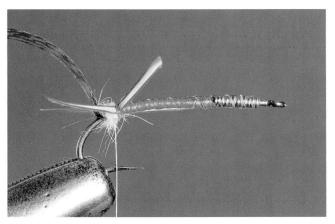

16. Select two fine tan goose biots and tie one on each side of the underbody to form the tails. The biots should be oriented so that they have opposite outward curvatures and extend backward. They should be the same length or slightly longer than the width of the hook gap. Trim the butts of the biot fibers.

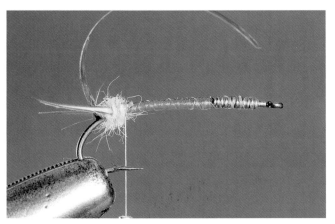

17. Dub a short section of the abdomen approximately the same length as the first dubbing ball.

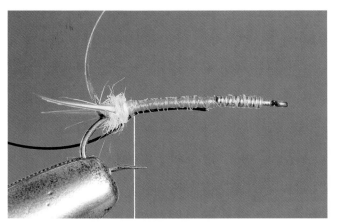

18. Wrap the tying thread forward to the front end of the telecom wire and tie in a length of brown D-Rib along the underside of the underbody, wrapping back to the dubbing.

19. Dub the abdomen with creamy yellow Awesome Possum, stopping at the midpoint of the hook. Be sure to keep the dubbing level.

20. Pull the Thin Skin forward over the abdomen and secure. Trim off the excess.

21. Wrap the D-Rib forward. The turns should be spaced approximately the same width as the D-Rib. Tie off the D-Rib.

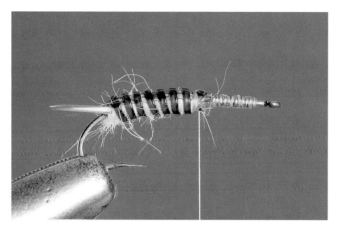

22. Trim the excess with your fingernail clippers.

23. Cut another strip of Thin Skin equal to the hook gap in width. Cut the strip across the width of the sheet. Tie in the strip by its end with the shiny side up and pointing back over the body.

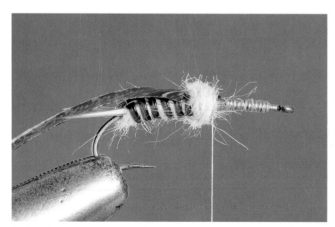

24. Apply creamy yellow Awesome Possum Dubbing and make the first segment of the thorax. The dubbing should be approximately twice the diameter of the abdomen and be ¼ the length of the remaining open hook shank.

25. Select a hen pheasant feather from the back region of the skin and cut a notch in the feather, removing the tip. Stroke the fibers at the base of the feather back on each side of the stem so that six to eight fibers remain on each side. The same feather can be used to make all three leg sets.

26. Place the feather over the top of the hook so that it straddles the first thorax section. Pinch the fibers of the hackle against the sides of the thorax with your left forefinger and thumb and take one loose turn of thread completely around them. Pull the thread taut and take several more turns to anchor them. The legs should be ½ the length of the hook. Trim the excess feather closely and keep the remaining feather for the next two leg steps.

27. Fold the first wing case forward. Do not pull it. Hold the strip tight against the thorax and secure it with a few turns of tying thread. Do not trim off the surplus strip.

28. Fold the Thin Skin strip back over the first wing case and secure it in this position, with the thread wraps directly over those that tied down the first wing case. Cut a V notch in the tip of the hen pheasant feather to create a new section of legs and repeat the previous sequences to make the next segment of the thorax, legs, and wing case.

29. Cut a V notch in the tip of the hen pheasant feather to create the third set of legs and repeat the previous sequences to make the third segment of the thorax, legs, and wing case.

30. An overhead view of the thorax section with three wing cases and sets of legs. Note the legs at each segment are the same length and the wing cases overlap the previous ones slightly, like roof shingles.

31. Trim the remaining wing case material.

32. Cut a third strip of Thin Skin approximately ⅔ the width of the hook gap and tie it in directly behind the hook eye. The shiny side should be facing up and the strip pointing past the hook eye. Press the strip against the top of the hook eye and take one loose turn of thread around it. Pull the thread tight to pinch down the width of the strip and anchor it in position. Trim off the butt end of the strip if necessary and take several more turns to secure it.

33. Dub a head with the same dubbing material. The diameter should be equal to the thorax segments and the thread should now be between the head and the third wing case segment.

34. Pull the Thin Skin strip back over the head tightly and bind it in place with a few turns of thread.

35. Trim the surplus Thin Skin closely.

36. Select two fine tan goose biots and tie one in along the side of the head with one turn of thread to form an antenna. The biot should curve away from the head.

37. Add the second biot on the opposite side of the head with a turn of thread. The antennae should be the same length or slightly shorter than the tail and curve outward. If the biots are small, I often use tweezers to hold them. Adjust the length to even them out if necessary and secure with two more turns of thread and trim off the surplus fibers closely. Whip-finish at the point where the antennae were tied in. Tint the tails and antennae with dark brown marker.

38. An overhead view of the finished nymph. The techniques used here result in a pattern with defined features without going to extremes. It lacks the inherent stiffness of many stonefly nymph imitations, which often causes them to be quickly rejected by the trout. The finished fly has a broad flattened appearance and the dark top and light underside typical of most stonefly nymphs.

GIANT BLACK
(*Pteronarcys* spp.)

Hook:	#4-8 Tiemco 200
Thread:	Black 8/0 Uni-Thread
Tails:	Dark brown goose biots
Abdomen:	Dark brown Stonefly Life Cycle dubbing
Rib:	Dark brown D-Rib
Thorax:	Same as abdomen
Legs:	Hen ring-necked pheasant back feather dyed dark brown
Wing Cases:	Mottled oak Thin Skin
Head:	Same as abdomen
Antennae:	Same as tails

GOLDEN
(*Acroneuria* spp., *Paragnetina immarginata*)

Hook:	#6-8 Tiemco 200
Thread:	Tan 8/0 Uni-Thread
Tails:	Yellowish tan goose biots, colored with dark brown Prismacolor marker
Abdomen:	Yellowish tan Harrop CEN Nymph Dubbing or golden yellow (stonefly) Life Cycle dubbing
Rib:	Dark brown D-Rib
Thorax:	Same as abdomen
Legs:	Hen ring-necked pheasant feather dyed wood duck
Wing Cases:	Mottled oak Thin Skin
Head:	Yellowish tan Harrop CEN Dubbing
Antennae:	Same as tails

ISOPERLA
(*Isoperla bilineata*)

Hook:	#14 Tiemco 200
Thread:	Light cahill 8/0 Uni-Thread
Tails:	Yellowish tan goose biots
Abdomen:	Creamy yellow Awesome Possum Dubbing and lemon wood-duck flank
Rib:	Fine gold wire
Thorax:	Same as abdomen
Legs:	Brown mottled partridge hackle
Wing Cases:	Mottled oak Thin Skin
Head:	Creamy yellow dubbing
Antennae:	Same as tails

EARLY BLACK
(*Capnia* spp.)

Hook:	#10-14 Tiemco 200
Thread:	Black 8/0 Uni-Thread
Tails:	Black goose biots
Abdomen:	Black (stonefly) Life Cycle dubbing
Rib:	Black D-Rib
Thorax:	Same as abdomen
Legs:	Hen ring-necked pheasant back feather dyed black
Wing Cases:	Mottled oak Thin Skin
Head:	Black dubbing
Antennae:	Same as tails

15

The Little Yellow Stoneflies

"She's a pretty insect, graceful and unhurried in flight, and when she dips down to the water to lay her eggs she is equally attractive to the trout."

CHAUNCY LIVELY, *CHAUNCY LIVELY'S FLYBOX*

My first exposure to the small, yellow-colored stoneflies of *Isoperla bilineata*, or the Yellow Sally, came many years ago during my teen years in the mountains of northern Pennsylvania on Kettle Creek. Kettle Creek flows nestled in the deep folds of the Black Forest Mountains of Potter County in north central Pennsylvania. The Kettle's steep mountain valley was the scene of extensive logging at the end of the nineteenth century, and the virgin hemlock, white pine, and hardwood stands were cut clear to supply the rapidly growing cities of the East Coast. The lumberjacks' crosscut saws and double-bit axes swept over the mountains of north central Pennsylvania like a brush fire consuming nearly all of the standing timber, moving from area to area, and leaving behind a barren landscape that would take many years to heal.

Today the forests have regenerated but still show faint scars from the lumber era boom, with log slides cut into the mountain edges and railroad grades still visible to the trained eye coursing the wooded valleys where the

Isoperla bilineata, *more commonly known as the Little Yellow Stonefly or the Yellow Sally, offers good fishing opportunities. Many Western streams have a cousin species* **Isoperla mormona,** *which is commonly referred to as the Mormon Girl.*

Above: Kettle Creek near Cross Fork, Pennsylvania, and its tributary streams Cross Fork Creek, Hammersley Fork, Little Kettle Creek, and the Germania Branch have good populations of Little Yellow Stoneflies. Pine Creek and its tributaries Slate Run and Cedar Run also have excellent hatches.

A wild brook trout caught on a mountain stream. The Little Yellow Stonefly is an effective searching pattern on small streams. BARRY AND CATHY BECK

narrow-gauge Shay locomotives of the Lackawanna Lumber Company pulled their log cars and Barnhart loaders along the steep cuts and switchbacks of the tight valley. Relics of the past still can be found in the form of discarded ax heads, log chains, and railroad spikes rusting away in the shade of the quiet woods.

The once sprawling boomtown of Cross Fork, with a population of over 1,500 residents, declined nearly as rapidly as it grew and is now only a tiny village of several dozen full-time residents. The little river once home to native brook trout was nearly decimated by the greed of the lumber barons' axes and saws and would take many years for the valley to return to a natural state. The native trout would be pushed into the headwater streams of Hammersley Fork, Cross Fork Creek, Windfall, the Little Kettle, and the Germania Branch. Fortunately the mountains and valleys have healed well with the passage of time and are once again home to black bear, bobcat, whitetail deer, and trout. The populations of wild brook trout never returned to the little river and were replaced by European brown trout, which thrive today, creating an often spectacular fishery with most of the classic eastern fly hatches and creating an abundance of opportunities to challenge anglers.

On that June day when Charley Brown and I pulled on our waders and rigged our rods, the excitement alone was nearly more than a teenaged boy could stand. It was my first fly-fishing trip to the north woods of Potter County and my first baptism in the cold waters of Kettle. The evening sun was still high in the sky when the first hatching *Isoperla* stoneflies began to appear and the brown trout began to feed aggressively on them. The pale yellow flies skipped across the surface in their attempts to become airborne and were taken greedily with splashy rises of the hungry fish as dozens of trout began to work the hatch steadily until darkness overtook the valley and the Kettle once again flowed quietly. Our evening was one of both frustration and futility as neither Charley nor I had any suitable imitations in our boxes to match them.

The following morning we went to the local fly shop to find flies to match the stoneflies that had frustrated us the prior evening and found only variations of the Adams tied with yellow bodies, which were poor imitations at best. The flies worked with limited success but were refused by fish in calmer waters that had more time to inspect our offerings. In those days Catskill-style dry flies still dominated most fishermen's fly boxes, and it would be several years before down-wing imitations would begin to gain acceptance. My initial reaction to the problem of the Yellow Sallies was to more closely match the color of the naturals by toning down the body color to more of a butter yellow, and replace the traditional Adams hackle recipe of brown and grizzly with a lighter mixture of pale ginger and chinchilla. These flies worked well in the riffles and pocketwaters but still did not work over difficult fish in quieter currents. The gradual acceptance of down-wing imitations and new materials suited to tie workable flat-wing styles would trigger the next phase of my experimentation with adult stonefly imitations.

The inspiration came to me one afternoon in the 1980s when I was spending a few days as a guest at the Texas Blockhouse Fish and Game Club in northern Pennsylvania, where my longtime friend Charley Brown worked as a warden and caretaker. The clubhouse is perched on the edge of a hill overlooking two small streams that flow on either side of it: Texas Creek on one side and Blockhouse Run on the opposite, which join downstream from the clubhouse to form the Little Pine Creek. The club has a long and rich history of serious outdoorsmen, including Herbert Hoover, and has miles of superb trout water.

We had spent the morning on the club water, where I had caught one of the stoneflies and spent some time studying the form of the insect, and the solution to a longstanding problem of imitating the little stones flashed through my mind. Fortunately I had brought my tying kit along. A good imitation needed to match the coloration closely, but more importantly it needed to sit close to the surface and float on top in broken water. The fly also needed to be more robust than a mayfly dun pattern and have the low, flat wing profile of the natural insect. At the kitchen table, I quickly dressed the fly that I would fish for the next twenty years with great success. The Z-Lon underwing sparkles as sunlight passes through it, and the elk hair provides enough stiffness in the wing to help keep the Z-Lon fibers flat over the fly's body to preserve the wing profile and improve floatation. Trimming the light ginger hackle flush on the underside of the hook allows the fly to float low in the film for selective fish. I made several more of the new pattern and tucked them into my fly box, eager to try them the next day.

The next morning, Charley and I were on a stretch of the stream where the bedrock ledges at the foot of the mountain valley turned the course of the currents in an abrupt hairpin turn, which fanned out into a flat pool. The far edge of the pool was retained by an old wooden cribbing wall, and a few low trees overhung and shaded its depths. The morning mist was just beginning to lift from the water's surface when I strung the little rod, fitting a light leader to the tip of the fly line, and finally one of the new yellow stonefly imitations, well greased with a floatant paste. The calm currents were broken from time to time with the soft rises of fish beginning to work a mixture of flies, and several fish were rising regularly. The first fish in this stretch occupied the tail out of the pool. I cautiously crept into position below and across from the trout and worked out enough line to reach it. The little stonefly pattern settled on the surface quietly several feet above his position, and the fish came lazily to the fly when its drift reached him. The new stonefly imitation disappeared in a quiet swirl, and the fish bolted when it felt the sting of the hook. I worked the brown carefully to the side to keep him from moving up the pool and putting down the other fish. After resting the pool for several minutes, I cast to the next fish, which was holding tight against the cribbing wall, and the stonefly gently dropped in his drift lane. Again, the fish took the fly without hesitation. I handed Charley a few flies, and we spent the rest of the morning enjoying success with the new pattern, beginning what would be a long stretch of similar successes with the pattern.

The yellow stoneflies of the *Isoperla* genus inhabit many of our smaller eastern freestone streams with gravel

*The Lime Sally (*Isoperla imbecilla*) is a closely related stonefly species that is often found in the same streams as the Little Yellow Stoneflies.*

bottoms, clean water, and high levels of dissolved oxygen. The nymphs live in the crevices between stones where they feed on smaller organisms. These small stoneflies enjoy a long emergence period, often showing on the water from mid-May well throughout much of the summer in the East, as well as in many Western states. The adult flies are a yellowish color overall, often exhibiting a greenish cast, and the wings are held flat over the back and extend past the abdomen when at rest. The stonefly has short legs, and as a result sits very close to the surface of the water, with most of the body in contact with the film, which produces a different light pattern on the surface of the water than that of a mayfly dun. The females are slightly larger than the males, measuring 12 to 14 mm, while the males average 10 to 12 mm. Both sexes are well matched with patterns tied on 2X long dry-fly hooks in sizes 14 and 16. In low water conditions where fish tend to be more skittish I use size 18 hooks.

Emergences are often nocturnal, and Ernest Schwiebert's later release of *Nymphs* as well as *Stoneflies* by Doug Swisher, Carl Richards, and Fred Arbona present these hatches as being a nighttime activity. While this is generally true, I have witnessed hatches of these flies during

evening hours on a number of streams as well as sporadic hatches throughout the day. Egg-laying activity brings the adults back to the stream and creates another opportunity to fish imitations of them. The flies typically hatch sporadically but can from time to time hatch in numbers significant enough to induce strong rises in the fish. Due to the emergence patterns of these yellow stones, the trout never seem to become highly selective toward them, but they are fond of the flies and take them whenever the opportunity presents itself. Because of this, I often search the water with a Little Yellow Stonefly when nothing is hatching. Our days on the water are too limited by life's demands to waste the middle portion of the day, and fishing a search pattern can often provide a satisfying way to optimize fishing time, especially in pocketwater and riffles. My favorite technique to fish these flies is with a 7½- to 9-foot leader, depending on the stream's size, tapered to a 5X tippet, and with the fly presented in the drift lanes between stones in the pocketwater and the seams where slower and faster currents meet, and drifted over any likely looking holding lies. Fish in these types of water will often rush the fly provided the drift is good, and the rises are usually fast paced.

TYING THE LITTLE YELLOW STONEFLY

LITTLE YELLOW STONEFLY

Hook:	#14-18 Daiichi 1260 or equivalent 2XL dry fly
Thread:	Light cahill 8/0 Uni-Thread
Tails:	Stiff pale ginger hackle barbs
Body:	Sulphur yellow Superfine dubbing
Wing:	Light gold or light yellow Z-Lon and bleached deer hair
Thorax:	Sulphur yellow Superfine dubbing
Hackle:	Pale ginger in open turns, clipped flat on the bottom
Head:	Sulphur yellow Superfine dubbing

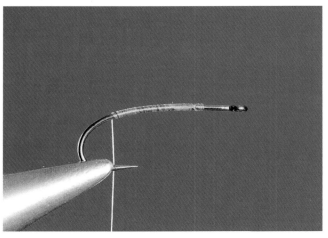

1. Clamp a 2XL dry-fly hook in the vise and attach light cahill 8/0 thread near the midpoint of the hook shank. Wrap the thread toward the bend of the hook, stopping at a point over the end of the barb.

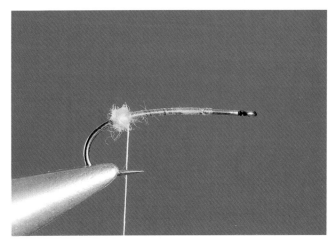

2. Make a very small ball of Superfine dubbing on the thread and wrap onto the hook.

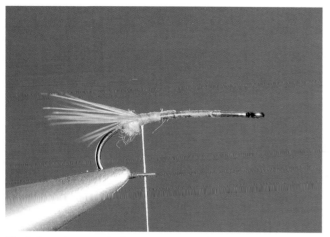

3. Select 8 to 10 light ginger hackle barbs and tie them in at a point ¹⁄₁₆ inch in front of the dubbing ball, being careful to keep them on top of the hook shank. Wrap back toward the base of the dubbing ball. The fibers should be divided into two equal groups on the sides of the dubbing ball.

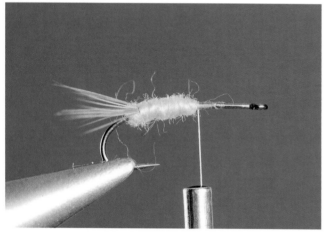

4. Dub a body that is even and equal to two-thirds of the hook-shank length.

5. Tie in an underwing of pale yellow Z-Lon that extends just past the hook bend. Trim the butts of the yarn closely.

6. Select a bunch of short, fine, bleached elk or deer hair.

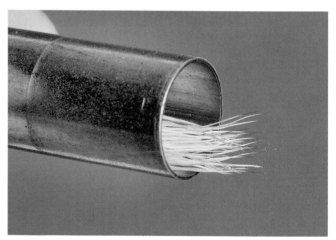

7. The size of the hair, when compressed, should be approximatly one third the diameter of a pencil. Remove all of the under hair and short hair from the bunch and even out the tips in a hair stacker.

8. Hold the wing hair on top of the hook shank. The tips of the hair should extend just beyond the underwing.

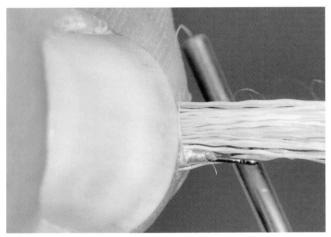

9. Grasp the bundle of wing hair with your left thumb and forefinger and pinch the hair snugly against the top of the body. Take a loose wrap of tying thread completely around the wing. Pull the thread taut in an upward direction while maintaining pressure on the wing with your left hand. Take several more turns of tying thread while maintaining your grasp on the wing.

10. The wing should look like this after you tie it in place. The hair should have only a small amount of flare.

11. Trim the butts of the wing hair closely.

12. Prepare a light ginger saddle hackle by stripping the webbed fibers from the base and tying in the hackle by the stem, leaving ⅛ inch of the stem exposed. Trim the excess hackle stem closely.

13. Dub a thorax, stopping at a point ¹⁄₁₆ inch from the hook eye.

15. Dub a small head and whip-finish. Trim the thread.

14. Wrap the hackle forward in open turns to the end of the thorax and tie it off. Trim off the excess hackle tip closely.

16. Rotate the vise jaws and trim the hackle fibers flat on the bottom. The resulting fly sits close to the surface film and has a very natural low-floating appearance.

16

All about Ants

If I were to make a selection of the most productive and consistent trout taking patterns of the terrestrials, I suppose it would have to be the ants.

ED KOCH, *TERRESTRIAL FISHING*

Years ago, when I had the time to fish without having the time to travel to a stream in a wilder setting, the Little Lehigh River filled my need. Flowing right through the heart of Allentown, and in close proximity to several other larger metropolitan areas, the Little Lehigh is a greenway oasis in the midst of all of that hustle and bustle of the increasingly urbanized and suburbanized East. While I would prefer to crawl on hands and knees through the shade of rhododendrons and hemlock to offer a dry fly to wild brook trout in a mountain

stream, the trout of the Little Lehigh do not come easily to the fly like those wild brookies do, and instead have a higher level of sophistication and selectivity conditioned by the pressure they see from the parade of fishermen who come to test them.

While I never fished this particular stream much in the earlier part of the season, I did fish the shaded banks a good bit in the summer and early fall as an escape from the heat and bright sun. Tall willows branch high above the water, reaching out over the currents of the long flat

Carpenter ants, some of the largest ant species found along trout streams, were the inspiration for some of the earliest ant imitations like the McCafferty and McMurray ants.

Penns Creek near Weikert, Pennsylvania, was the home river of writer Charles Wetzel, who fished sunken ant patterns extensively there. BARRY AND CATHY BECK

pools, and the trout that inhabit these flats cruise lazily looking for food. Among the branches are a variety of beetles, aphids, ants, and other terrestrial insects, which from time to time lose their footing in the trees and find their way onto the water and quite often into the stomachs of the trout below.

Of all of these, the ants are the most abundant and most active, being constantly on the move, gathering food or performing other activities as most colonized insect varieties do. While ants are active for much of the year, the heat of midsummer makes them more active than at other times of the year and more prone to becoming a meal for the trout that hold them in high regard. A gentle breeze or a gust of wind blows numbers of these terrestrial insects into the water, and the fish anticipate and enjoy the occasion. Mating swarms of flying ants present another opportunity that can often place hundreds of ants on the water at a time, and those fortunate to experience these occurrences witness one of fly fishing's great treats.

I remember a summer day years ago on the Little Lehigh when the weather was almost oppressively hot.

The morning dew was long gone and the cicadas were beginning to sing loudly in the trees. I was working my way quietly along the stream, being careful to stay well away from the edge of the water and keeping a low profile to avoid alerting the fish to my presence. A brown trout cruised along the edge of the bank under the willows, gliding slowly along and actively looking for food. From my fly box I chose a #14 McMurray Ant, which is a perfect imitation of a large carpenter ant, and knotted it carefully to the 6X tippet. I kept the cast low and presented the fly from a kneeling position to avoid spooking the fish, and the little rod put the fly quietly on the water five or six feet ahead of the trout's path with only the leader and a few feet of fly line on the water. As the fly touched the water, the fish sensed the vibration, rushed to the drifting ant, and then proceeded to drift with the fly for a foot or more while nervously inspecting it from only an inch or two below. Finally, the trout tipped up and in an almost lazy, yawning fashion inhaled the fly. That day was one of those magical days on the stream, and my journal shows that the same performance

Above: Red ants are common along many streams, usually in smaller sizes than darker ants. Trout can show preferences toward ant colors based on the varieties they commonly see. JAY NICHOLS

Ant imitations are important flies for limestone and freestone stream trout. During the hot summer months many ants fall into streams and trout grow fond of them. BARRY AND CATHY BECK

was repeated on that day almost forty times before darkness settled on the water. My fishing journal shows many similar days on the stream when an ant imitation saved the day, and my fly boxes always are well stocked with a good assortment of patterns, both wet and dry.

Ants belong to the family Formicidae and represent one of the largest groups of insect varieties found in nature. As a whole, ants and their cousin termites are estimated to make up between 15 and 25 percent of the earth's entire animal biomass. New species are constantly being identified and added to a growing list that already includes more than 8,800 individual species, with nearly 600 of those found in North America alone. The only parts of the world that do not have any indigenous ant species are Antarctica, Greenland, Iceland, and the Hawaiian Islands. Sizes of ants can vary from $\frac{1}{10}$ inch to nearly 1 inch in length; the color is usually cinnamon, red, black, or combinations of these shades. While it isn't important to be able to identify all the possible ant species we might encounter on the stream, it's important to understand the

Above: Ants play a huge role in the diets of many trout; your fly boxes should include a good assortment of patterns to match them in a range of sizes from 10 to 22 and tied in shades of black, cinnamon, red, and brown. JAY NICHOLS

A selection of the author's flying ant patterns tied with CDC to create a good wing profile and add movement to the fly. JAY NICHOLS

importance of these insects in the trout's diet and be prepared with fly patterns to match the local species, not only in the hot summer months, but throughout the entire fishing season.

From a fishing point of view, ants pose a challenging problem unlike most other stream situations, and that is identification. Ants seldom announce their presence on the water and drift for the most part undetected by fishermen due to the way that they sit tight to the surface film of the water. Vince Marinaro writes in *A Modern Dry Fly Code* about the frustration he had with his Letort trout in trying to determine what they were actively feeding upon in those periods where there were no obvious emergences of hatching flies or falling spinners. Getting answers to the question required closer investigation. In desperation he fashioned a makeshift seine to filter the surface film and was astonished at the number of minute insects, both aquatic and terrestrial that were captured in the mesh. His fishing that evening was focused on capturing a few fish to perform autopsies on to confirm

A meadow on the Letort Spring Run. Vince Marinaro writes in A Modern Dry Fly Code *of an episode where his frustration with rising trout inspires the construction of a seine to inspect the currents for drifting insects. The discovery of an abundance of tiny ants in the seine inspires the development of the first imitations of floating ants as well as other land-based insects.* BARRY AND CATHY BECK

his suspicions, and he found that the stomach contents of the trout captured comprised, among other things, a vast number of tiny ants and some larger ants in each fish studied.

From a fly-tying perspective, ants require a different approach as they differ in both silhouette and behavior from all of the other food organisms that the trout see. Unlike adult mayflies, stoneflies, and caddisflies that float, or other insect life-cycle stages that are submerged, the ant neither floats or sinks, but instead sits low in the surface film, allowing the fish to gain a clear view of the insect. This characteristic is significant when dressing imitations. But the ant's profile or silhouette is radically different from those of all other insects that live in or near the waters that harbor trout and commands our attention. The ant's body comprises three separate and distinct segments with each being connected to the next with thin areas. The long anterior segment called the "gaster" is robust and slightly larger in diameter than the

other body segments. The midsection or thorax is typically thin with the six legs connected at this point. The third body segment, the head, is also thick like the gaster. Fly tiers over the years have imitated ants in some unique ways, and much of the early work in developing effective imitations has its roots in the fertile limestone country of Pennsylvania.

The earliest pattern tied to specifically imitate an ant was created by a commercial tier named Bob McCafferty who created a simple pattern built from black tying silk in two segments (head and gaster) with a thin waist. These segments were saturated with head cement to mimic the glossy surface of the naturals, and the legs were imitated with a turn or two of soft black hackle. The McCafferty Ant was fished wet and was reported to be the single most effective fly pattern on Spring Creek in Bellefonte, Pennsylvania, and also was the fly of choice for Charles Wetzel on Penns Creek. I use the McCafferty-style ant with a great deal of success and also make these with the

Swarms of mating ants (flying ants) are an unpredictable occurrence that can trigger frenzied feeding when they fall in the water. Anglers should always carry a few patterns to be prepared for this event.

body sections dubbed from blackish-brown-colored Australian opossum. This is probably my favorite wet-fly pattern, especially in the early season, and is effective when the water is high or slightly off-colored.

The next ant imitation to come along was developed by Vince Marinaro to imitate the cinnamon-colored ants common on the Letort in Carlisle, Pennsylvania. Marinaro's pattern relies on horse hair dyed golden brown for the material to create the two body segments and for the tying thread itself. The legs were imitated with a blue-dun-colored hackle wound at the waist, and Marinaro comments in the introduction to the third print edition of *A Modern Dry Fly Code* in 1970 that "I was immensely impressed by the abundance of ants, in the meadows, on the water, and as revealed by the autopsies of trout. And truthfully, if I were to choose one pattern above all others, day in and day out, from fish to fish, the most enduring in its season, it would be the ant in its various sizes and colors." He goes on to say that "I could find nothing in American fly-tying literature to help me fashion a

good pattern of the ant. It seems to have been completely ignored by American Fishermen. British authors did not ignore the ant, but the tie recommended by Halford and others was unacceptable to me and to the trout. It looked exactly like any other upright-winged pattern of a mayfly. The first really sensible model of an ant that I saw was tied by the late McCafferty. . . . He never tied anything but a black pattern and always in large sizes, perhaps 10 or 12. He always tied them to sink, never to float, something which puzzled me exceedingly, for the ants do not sink but float well, even the large carpenter ants." Vince Marinaro certainly deserves credit for being the originator of the first floating-ant imitations.

The next innovation in the development of ant imitations was by yet another Pennsylvanian fly tier, the late Ed Sutryn. Ed was fishing one day near McMurray, Pennsylvania, in the early 1960s when he witnessed a frenzied feeding spree by the trout on large carpenter ants that were falling from the leaves of a large oak tree at the edge of the stream. Sutryn imitated these large flies with two small cylinders of balsa wood threaded onto a length of fine monofilament and dipped in black lacquer. The assembly was lashed to a fine-wire dry-fly hook in the center of the shank and a rooster hackle wound around its waist to imitate the legs. Sutryn exclusively fished a size 14 pattern, saying it was the only fly he needed. The beauty of the McMurray Ant is the way that it sits pressed into the surface film much like the natural ant, and even more importantly the way that it performs. By being constructed from wood, the fly is virtually unsinkable and does not require a number of false casts to flick the moisture from it in between casts. In the difficult limestone streams of Pennsylvania, you often get only one cast to a fish because trout are so spooky; therefore it is essential to minimize your movements. Over the years I've had tremendous success with the McMurray pattern and carry it in several colors and sizes, especially the larger ones.

In Ernest Schwiebert's *Trout* (1978), he describes three ant patterns and pictures them in the color plates. They are uniquely dressed to include all three separate body segments. Schwiebert preferred to use natural dubbing for the body segments, feeling that the materials would duplicate the natural's shiny wet exoskeleton. I too prefer a dubbed ant body as it lands on the surface lightly compared with those made from balsa wood or cork. In the 1984 second edition printing of *Trout,* Schwiebert discusses the development of Gary Borger's parachute-style ant imitation and explains that in his own fishing, he had made the transition to this style of dressing for all of his floating-ant imitations. The uniqueness of the Borger-style parachute ant is that it achieves an impression in the surface film much like the Marinaro and McMurray patterns by sitting low in that "neither floating or sinking" posture of a natural ant, and as a benefit lands much lighter on the water than the hard-bodied dressings. The Borger ants use a parachute post tied in at the forward section of the hook, and the tie-in point of the wing post or parachute post material is concealed by the dubbing of that body segment.

The ant imitation presented here is the result of many years of experimenting with a variety of imitations and a combination of the best qualities and design considerations that are critical to success on the stream over difficult fish. My ant uses the Borger-style parachute hackle to represent the legs of the ant and to support the fly in the film, but I move the parachute post to the center of the hook shank for better balance and to assure that the fly sits flat in the film. The parachute hackle, when placed forward of center, has more of a chance of tilting the fly at an unnatural angle and ruining the presentation. Moving the parachute post to the center creates the challenge of preserving the thin waistline of the natural ant, which is an important trigger image for the trout to key on. The key is to select only half of fibers you would usually use for the post and tie them in by the exact center of the material bundle, which should be about an inch long, with only one or two tight turns of thread. Once you bring the two ends together and wrap thread around the base, you have a solid post to wrap the hackle around and a bright spot (you can use any color) that will help you see the fly on the water. White makes a nice post that isn't objectionable but can be hard to see on water where there are bits of foam floating on the surface, and my ants usually have a post made from bright pink, orange, or chartreuse.

These ants are effective imitations and are worth your while to try. I make black, cinnamon, red, a carpenter ant imitation that has a chocolate brown head and a black gaster, and a red-headed ant that has been my favorite for years. I also make a flying-ant imitation in the black, cinnamon, and red-headed versions by adding a strip of pearlescent Mylar film at the center of the hook shank to represent the flat folded wings of the natural. Another good flying ant imitation eliminates the parachute post and hackle and incorporates a CDC wing—great for difficult fish in flat clear water. On the CDC ant patterns, I like to add three Midge Flash fibers tied at the midpoint of the hook shank with figure-eight wraps and trimmed to length to represent legs for an extra dose of realism.

TYING THE CDC FLYING ANT (CINNAMON)

CDC FLYING ANT (Cinnamon)

Hook:	#18-22 Daiichi 1180
Thread:	Rusty brown 8/0 Uni-Thread
Gaster:	Cinnamon caddis Superfine dubbing
Head:	Cinnamon caddis Superfine dubbing
Wings:	Natural dun CDC
Legs (optional):	Root beer Midge Flash

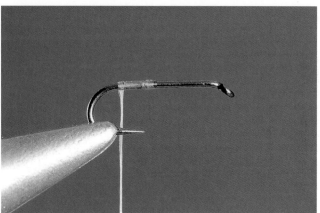

1. Clamp a fine-wire dry-fly hook in the vise and attach rusty brown 8/0 thread behind the midpoint. Wrap the tying thread toward the hook bend, stopping at a point over the end of the barb.

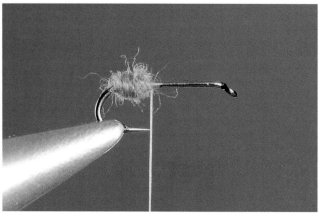

2. Apply cinnamon caddis Superfine dubbing to the thread and build a full gaster equal to one-third the hook length.

3. Wrap the tying thread to the midpoint of the hook shank. Attach three strands of root beer Midge Flash to the hook with figure-eight turns of thread.

4. Separate the legs with your fingers and wrap the thread between the fibers with figure eight turns to maintain the separation.

5. Select two natural dun CDC feathers and stack them with the tips evened. Tie the CDC feathers down on the top of the hook shank so that the tips extend just past the hook bend. Trim off the base of the feathers.

6. Wrap the tying thread to the hook eye, making sure to cover the base of the wing material.

7. Apply cinnamon caddis Superfine dubbing to the thread and build the head, starting at the eye and working back toward the center of the hook. The head should be slightly less than one-third of the hook length. Whip-finish and trim off the thread.

8. An overhead view of the finished ant. This technique makes tying small flying-ant patterns practical and results in a lifelike and effective pattern. A CDC wing negates the need for a wound hackle to support the fly in the film, and Midge Flash makes a realistic imitation of the legs and creates a well-defined light pattern for the trout.

TYING THE PARACHUTE ANT (RED-HEADED)

PARACHUTE ANT (Red-Headed)

Hook:	#14–20 Daiichi 1100
Thread:	Black 8/0 Uni-Thread
Gaster:	Black Superfine dubbing
Head:	Midge red Superfine dubbing
Post:	White or fluorescent colored yarn
Wings (optional):	Pearl Mylar strip tied flat over gaster
Hackle:	Dark dun

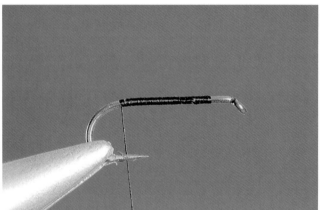

1. Clamp a dry-fly hook in the vise and attach black 8/0 thread at the midpoint of the hook. Wrap the thread toward the hook bend, stopping at a point over the end of the barb.

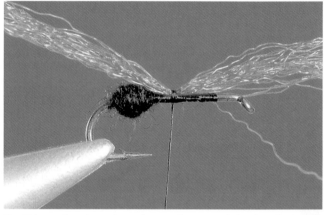

3. Wrap the thread to the midpoint of the hook. Cut a length of wing-post yarn of about 1½ inches and divide into halves with your dubbing needle. Bind a section of this at the midpoint of the center of the yarn.

2. Apply black Superfine dubbing and build a robust gaster approximately one-third of the hook length. The gaster should be slightly longer and larger in diameter than the head.

4. Take another tight turn of thread in the center of the yarn and bring the two ends of the yarn together over the hook. Take two tight turns in front of the post.

5. While holding the wing post upright, wrap around it upward for 1/16 inch and then back down, stopping on the hook shank in front of the post. I make one tight wrap around the hook and then wrap around the base of the post, first going upward on the post and then back down to lock them together and to stiffen this post base. The amount of wrapping over the post should vary proportionately with the size of the imitation to be tied. I will usually make the overwrap 1/16 inch on the smaller flies and slightly more on the larger ones.

6. Prepare a dark dun hackle by stripping away the webby fibers at its base and tie the hackle in by the stem in front of the wing. Orient the hackle so that the glossy side is facing up and leave a short length of clear stem exposed. Trim away the excess hackle stem and wrap the tying thread to the hook eye.

7. Apply midge red Superfine dubbing to the thread and build a small head, working your way back toward the post.

8. The head segment should be slightly less than one-third of the hook length.

9. Grip the hackle with your hackle pliers and make one open wrap to the top of the thread wraps on the post.

10. Wind the hackle back down the post in close turns.

11. Tie off the hackle close against the post. Trim the surplus hackle closely. Whip-finish the thread in front of the post and trim off.

12. Trim the post to length. This parachute technique permits the very thin waist in the center of the fly's body to successfully imitate the distinctive profile of an ant pressed in the film of the water. Moving the post to the center of the hook shank also allows the fly to sit level and more naturally.

PARACHUTE CARPENTER ANT

Hook: #10-14 Daiichi 1100
Thread: Black 8/0 Uni-Thread
Gaster: Black Superfine dubbing
Head: Mahogany brown Superfine dubbing
Post: White or fluorescent-colored yarn
Wings (optional): Pearl mylar strip tied flat over gaster
Hackle: Dark blue dun

PARACHUTE ANT (Black)

Hook: #14-22 Daiichi 1100
Thread: Black 8/0 Uni-Thread
Gaster: Black Superfine dubbing
Head: Black Superfine dubbing
Post: White or fluorescent-colored yarn
Wings (optional): Pearl Mylar strip tied flat over gaster
Hackle: Black

PARACHUTE ANT (Cinnamon)

Hook: #18-22 Daiichi 1180
Thread: Rusty brown 8/0 Uni-Thread
Gaster: Cinnamon caddis Superfine dubbing
Head: Cinnamon caddis Superfine dubbing
Post: White or fluorescent-colored yarn
Wings (optional): Pearl Mylar strip tied flat over gaster
Hackle: Ginger

PARACHUTE ANT (Red)

Hook:	#14-20 Daiichi 1100
Thread:	Red 8/0 Uni-Thread
Gaster:	Midge red Superfine dubbing
Head:	Midge red Superfine dubbing
Post:	White or fluorescent-colored yarn
Wings (optional):	Pearl Mylar strip tied flat over gaster
Hackle:	Dark dun

CDC FLYING CARPENTER ANT

Hook:	#10-14 Daiichi 1100
Thread:	Black 8/0 Uni-Thread
Gaster:	Black Superfine dubbing
Head:	Mahogany brown Superfine dubbing
Wings:	Natural dun CDC
Legs (optional):	Black Midge Flash

CDC FLYING ANT (Black)

Hook:	#14-20 Daiichi 1100
Thread:	Black 8/0 Uni-Thread
Gaster:	Black Superfine dubbing
Head:	Black Superfine dubbing
Wings:	Natural dun CDC
Legs (optional):	Black Midge Flash

CDC FLYING ANT (Red-Headed)

Hook: #14–20 Daiichi 1100
Thread: Black 8/0 Uni-Thread
Gaster: Black Superfine dubbing
Head: Midge Red Superfine dubbing
Wings: Natural dun CDC
Legs (optional): Black Midge Flash

CDC FLYING ANT (Red)

Hook: #14–20 Daiichi 1100
Thread: Red 8/0 Uni-Thread
Gaster: Midge red Superfine dubbing
Head: Midge red Superfine dubbing
Wings: Natural dun CDC
Legs (optional): Root beer Midge Flash

PARACHUTE FLYING ANT (Black)

Hook: #14–22 Daiichi 1100
Thread: Black 8/0 Uni-Thread
Gaster: Black Superfine dubbing
Head: Black Superfine dubbing
Post: Yarn
Wings: Pearl Embossed Flashback strip
Hackle: Black

PARACHUTE FLYING ANT (Cinnamon)

Hook:	#18-22 Daiichi 1180
Thread:	Rusty brown 8/0 Uni-Thread
Gaster:	Cinnamon caddis Superfine dubbing
Head:	Cinnamon caddis Superfine dubbing
Post:	White or fluorescent colored yarn
Wings:	Pearl Embossed Flashback strip
Hackle:	Ginger

MCCAFFERTY-STYLE WET ANT

Hook:	#10-20 Daiichi 1550
Thread:	Black 8/0 Uni-Thread
Body:	Two sections of dark blackish dubbing with a thin waist between the segments
Hackle:	Two turns of natural black hen hackle

Note: The original McCafferty patterns had gasters and heads made of two pronounced segments of tying thread coated with several applications of black lacquer. The gaster or abdominal section should be longer than the head.

Bibliography

Arbona, Fred L., Jr. *Mayflies, the Angler, and the Trout.* Tulsa, OK: Winchester, 1980.

Bergman, Ray. *Trout.* New York: Knopf, 1938.

Buckland, John. *The Simon and Schuster Pocket Guide to Trout and Salmon Flies.* New York: Simon and Schuster, 1986.

Caucci, Al, and Bob Nastasi. *Hatches.* New York: Comparahatch, 1975.

———. *Fly Tyer's Color Guide.* New York: Comparahatch, 1977.

Cross, Reuben. *Fur, Feathers, and Steel.* New York: Dodd, Mead, 1940.

Dunne, J. W. *Sunshine and the Dry Fly.* London: A. C. Black, 1924.

Edwards, Oliver. *Flytyers Masterclass.* Wayne, NJ: Stoeger, 1995.

Flick, Arthur. *Streamside Guide to Naturals and Their Imitations.* New York: Putnam's Sons, 1947. Reprint, New York: Crown, 1970.

Fox, Charles K. *This Wonderful World of Trout.* Harrisburg, PA: Telegraph, 1963. Reprinted as *Rising Trout.* Carlisle, PA: Foxcrest, 1967.

Halford, Frederic M. *Floating Flies and How to Dress Them.* London, 1886.

———. *Dry Fly Fishing in Theory and Practice.* London, 1889.

———. *Dry Fly Entomology.* London, 1897.

———. *Modern Development of the Dry Fly.* London, 1910.

Harrop, René. *Trout Hunter.* Boulder, CO: Pruett Publishing, 2003.

Hewitt, Edward R. *Telling on the Trout.* New York: Scribner, 1926.

Humphreys, Joe. *Trout Tactics.* Harrisburg, PA: Stackpole, 1981.

Jennings, Preston J. *A Book of Trout Flies.* New York: Derrydale, 1935. Reprint, New York: Crown, 1970.

Jorgensen, Poul. *Modern Fly Dressings for the Practical Angler.* New York: Winchester, 1976.

Kaufmann, Randall. *The Fly Tyer's Nymph Manual.* Portland, OR: Western Fisherman's Press, 1986.

Koch, Ed. *Terrestrial Fishing.* Harrisburg, PA: Stackpole, 1990.

LaBranche, George M. L. *The Dry Fly and Fast Water.* New York: Scribner, 1914.

LaFontaine, Gary. *The Dry Fly: New Angles.* Helena, MT: Greycliffe, 1990.

Leisenring, James E., and Vernon S. Hidy. *The Art of Tying the Wet Fly and Fishing the Flymph.* New York: Crown, 1971.

Leiser, Eric. *Fly Tying Materials.* New York: Crown, 1973.

———. *The Metz Book of Hackle.* New York: Nick Lyons, 1987.

Lively, Chauncy. *Chauncy Lively's Flybox: A Portfolio of Modern Trout Flies.* Harrisburg, PA: Stackpole Books, 1980.

McClane, A. J. *McClane's Standard Fishing Encyclopedia and International Angling Guide.* New York: Holt, Rinehart & Winston, 1953.

Marinaro, Vincent C. *A Modern Dry Fly Code.* New York: Putnam's Sons, 1950. Reprint, New York: Crown, 1970.

———. *In The Ring of The Rise.* New York: Crown, 1976.

Migel, J. Michael, and Leonard M. Wright Jr. *The Masters on the Nymph.* New York: Doubleday, 1979.

Nemes, Sylvester. *The Soft Hackled Fly Addict.* Chicago, IL: Nemes, 1981.

Pritt, T. E. *Yorkshire Trout Flies.* N.p.: Leeds, 1885.

———. *North Country Flies.* London, 1886.

Proper, Datus C. *What the Trout Said.* New York: Knopf, 1982. Reprint, New York: Lyons & Burford, 1989.

Quick, Jim. *Trout Fishing and Trout Flies.* New York: Castle, 1957.

Schwiebert, Ernest G. *Matching the Hatch.* New York: Macmillan, 1955.

———. *Remembrances of Rivers Past.* New York: Macmillan, 1972.

———. *Nymphs.* New York: Winchester, 1973.

———. *Trout.* 2nd ed. New York: Dutton, 1984.

———. *Death of a Riverkeeper.* New York: Dutton, 1980.

————. *A River for Christmas.* New York: Penguin Group, 1988.

————. *The Complete Schwiebert.* New York: Penguin Group, 1990.

Shenk, Ed. *Fly Rod Trouting.* Harrisburg, PA: Stackpole, 1989.

Skues, George E. M. *Minor Tactics of the Chalkstream.* London, 1910.

————. *The Way of a Trout with a Fly.* London, 1921.

————. *Nymph Fishing for Chalkstream Trout.* London, 1939.

Solomon, Larry, and Eric Leiser. *The Caddis and the Angler.* Harrisburg, PA: Stackpole, 1977.

Stalcup, Shane. *Mayflies Top to Bottom.* Portland, OR: Frank Amato, 2002.

Sturgis, William B. *Fly Tying.* New York: Scribner, 1940.

Swisher, Doug, and Carl Richards. *Selective Trout.* New York : Crown, 1971.

Talleur, Dick. *The Versatile Fly Tyer.* New York: Lyons & Burford, 1990.

Theodore Gordon Fly Fishers. *American Trout Fishing.* New York: Knopf, 1965.

Wetzel, Charles M. *Trout Flies, Naturals, and Imitations.* Harrisburg, PA: Stackpole, 1955.

Additional References to *Isonychia* Species

Funk, David H., and Bernard W. Sweeney. "Evidence for Reproductive Isolation between Two 'Forms' of Isonychai bicolor (Walker) (Ephemeroptera: Isonychiidae)." North American Benthological Society, 1992. Stroud Water Research Center, Academy of Natural Sciences, Avondale, PA.

Kondratieff, Boris C., and J. Reese Voshell Jr. "North and Central American Species of *Isonychia* (Ephemeroptera: Oligoneuriidae)." From the *Transactions of the Entomological Society*, Volume 110: 129-244, 1984.

Sweeney, Bernard W. "Bioenergetic and Developmental Response of a Mayfly to Thermal Variation." Stroud Water Research Center, Academy of Natural Sciences of Philadelphia, and Department of Biology, University of Pennsylvania, Philadelphia. American Society of Limnology and Oceanography, 1978.

Additional References to *Isoperla bilineata*

Carl Richards, Doug Swisher, and Fred L. Arbona. *Stoneflies.* New York: Nick Lyons Books, 1980.

Ernest G. Schwiebert. *Nymphs.* Vol. 2, *Stoneflies, Caddisflies, and Other Important Insects.* Guilford, CT: Globe Pequot, 2007.

Index